Letters to a Fiction Writer

Also by Frederick Busch . . .

Letters to a Fiction Writer

edited by Frederick Busch

W. W. Norton & Company
New York • London

The text of this book is composed in Usherwood Book
With the display set in Mramor CS
Composition by Platinum Manuscript Services
Manufacturing by The Maple-Vail Book Manufacturing Group
Book design by Lane Kimball Trubey

Library of Congress Cataloging-in-Publication Data

Letters to a fiction writer / edited by Frederick Busch.
p.   cm.
Includes bibliographical references.
ISBN 0-393-04735-0
1. Fiction—Authorship. 2. Authors, American—20th century—correspondence.
I. Busch, Frederick, 1941–
PN3355.L38   1999
808.3—dc21   98-54320
CIP

W. W. Norton & Company, Inc., 500 Fifth Avenue, New York, N.Y. 10110
http://www.wwnorton.com

W. W. Norton & Company Ltd., 10 Coptic Street, London WC1A 1PU

1 2 3 4 5 6 7 8 9 0

Contents

Note

The editor is responsible for flaws, omissions, mistakes, and misconceptions readers may find in this book.

Although he will have committed his share of errors, the editor has, on the other hand, been at all successful because he was blessed by the patience and assistance of members of the writing community, acknowledging whom—while absolving them from any share in his gaffes—is a pleasure: Sally Fitzgerald, who offered wise counsel and active assistance; Pam Durban, my good friend; Linck Johnson of Colgate's Department of English; David Hughes, Head of Reference at Colgate's Case Library; the Colgate University Research Council; Christina Licursi; Elise Vogel, good writer and good friend; David Jauss, longtime amigo; Dan Chaon; David Markson.

A sweeping salute to Jill Bialosky of W. W. Norton, who was seized by the first glimmers of this book in the bar of the Colgate Inn, where all we drank was mineral water and all we discussed was how, in our writing, to talk straight.

—FB

Letters to a Fiction Writer

Frederick Busch

Introduction

Dear Sir:

It has been quite awhile since I received, but failed to answer, your reply to the novel I sent for your consideration.

I was twenty-five or twenty-six, and I had already perpetrated two and one-half novels. (The half, a runty pastiche of Malamud *and* Faulkner—truly—constituted my first, tottering steps.) Editors at a number of houses had been very kind to me, and had written of their sorrow when my manuscripts did not appeal to their colleagues. A writer passing through Colgate had suggested that I send my book to his agent (and then had sped on, before I could press my brilliant work upon the writer himself). You were his agent. Perhaps you still are. I sent you the best letter I could compose, begging you to read my novel, telling you what I thought then were the fresh, vivid, exciting stories of my near-misses with several houses. You responded at once, and with hospitality: I was welcome to send my manuscript.

I waited the usual six centuries for a reply, and I performed the usual tricks: I called your office and rang off when my courage failed. I awaited the mailman on our front porch, and then at the corner of our street and, at last, on *his* front porch. And then, when the Ganges had filled with opals and the Hudson had turned to Bâtard-Montrachet, up our walk came the postman, edging warily toward me perhaps because I was snuffling and sidling and tipping over with anxiety. Maybe he knew that I saw him holding out letters, but no padded envelope containing a manuscript that someone did not feel "we can optimistically represent."

Well, the manuscript did come the next day. You sent it, you noted, "under separate cover." What you sent first, with a nice sense of timing, was your letter of rejection. You did not employ euphemisms about my self-obsessed characters or dumb plot or gassy prose. You did not, on the other hand, suggest that I could actually compose narrative fiction or that my work possessed some promise. You said only what you knew needed saying. This is the entirety of your note:

> Dear Mr. Busch:
>   Ah, if only you wrote fiction as well as you write letters
> of inquiry.

And you signed with regret, which was not, may I say, quite so sizable as my own. I regretted my inquiry letter, I regretted writing fiction (or whatever it was I had written) and I regretted that we weren't face-to-face. I fantasized about modes of delivering violence to the person. I considered weeping in the weak sunlight of early spring on Payne Street in Hamilton, New York.

However, I went inside and I sulked. I pouted for Judy, my wife, who came home after a day of teaching in a rural elementary school. She might be fatigued, I pointed out, but *I* was, after the agonies of inventing a character just like me who suffered existential crises not unlike my own, humiliated and rejected and inconsolable and failed.

She had been coping with third graders until half an hour before, so it took no major changing of gears for her to comfort me. And, soon enough, I was muleheadedly writing more fiction, more letters to publishers and agents, complaints to my friends who had, only the day before, sent me letters about *their* out-of-the-typewriter experiences with publishers and agents. If one has talent—and it is the vastest of assumptions, is it not?—then the next necessity is energy: the energy to find and sustain story—that vivid and continuous dream about which John Gardner taught. It is an energy, sir, that permits one to receive letters such as yours, and to sustain the damage they do, and then to return to all that darkness, and the little pool of light within it where one works. As Hemingway's heroic gambler tells us in "The Gambler, the Nun, and the Radio," one can only "continue, slowly, and wait for luck to change."

But, sir, the pain was real. I still feel it, a little. But I've never forgotten, either, the wonderful letters I did receive—from Esther Yntema at Atlantic–Little, Brown or from Frank Brunotts at Hill & Wang. Robert Nye, the poet, novelist, and critic who now lives in Ireland, cabled me, about a year after I had your letter, from Scotland: CALDER ACCEPTS YOUR NOVEL. CONGRATULATIONS! Without telling me, he had recommended my novel, sent for his critique, to his publisher and so, for about $480, I sold my novel to the English publishers of Samuel Beckett and Henry Miller. Robert had sustained me for years with his own horror stories, and with his unabated drive to write well in a world essentially inhospitable to prose that kicked and twisted on the page.

If there are always letters from people such as yourself, sir, there are, also, letters from people like Robert Nye. They arrive, in fact, from such people—do you believe it?—as Anton Chekhov, who, grumbling and scolding, nevertheless makes time to offer this advice to a new writer:

> In my opinion, descriptions of nature should be extremely brief and offered by the way, as it were. Give up commonplaces, such as: "the setting sun, bathing in the waves of the darkening sea, flooded with purple gold," and so on. Or: "Swallows flying over the surface of the water chirped gaily." In descriptions of nature one should seize

upon minutiae, grouping them so that when, having read the passage, you close your eyes, a picture is formed. For example, you will evoke a moonlit night by writing that on the mill dam the glass fragments of a broken bottle flashed like a bright little star, and that the black shadow of a dog or a wolf rolled along like a ball."[1]

F. Scott Fitzgerald, perhaps even busier and more harried than yourself, sir, returned a short story to a sophomore at Radcliffe with these admonitions: "I'm afraid the price for doing professional work is a good deal higher than you are prepared to pay at present," he begins. And then he instructs:

> It was necessary for Dickens to put into Oliver Twist the child's passionate resentment at being abused and starved that had haunted his whole childhood. Ernest Hemingway's first stories "In Our Time" went right down to the bottom of all that he had ever felt and known. In "This Side of Paradise" I wrote about a love affair that was still bleeding as fresh as the skin wound on a haemophile. . . . That . . . is the price of admission. Whether you are prepared to pay it or, whether it coincides or conflicts with your attitude on what is "nice" is something for you to decide. . . . You wouldn't be interested in a soldier who was only a LITTLE brave.[2]

William Faulkner, like Fitzgerald, suggests what it takes to write serious fiction; in addition, like Chekhov, he grapples with some of the inner workings of the endeavor:

[1] Anton Chekhov to A. P. Chekhov, May 10, 1886, in *The Letters of Anton Chekhov*, trans. Avrahm Yarmolinsky (New York: Viking, 1968).

[2] F. Scott Fitzgerald to Frances Turnbull, November 9, 1938, in *F. Scott Fitzgerald: A Life in Letters,* ed. Matthew J. Bruccoli, (New York: Scribner's, 1994).

You are learning. All you need is to agonise and sweat over it, never be quite satisfied even when you know it is about as right as it can be humanly made, never to linger over it when done because you dont have time, you must hurry hurry to write it again and better, the best this time. Not the same story over again, but Joan Williams, who has the capacity to suffer and anguish and would trade it for nothing under heaven. . . . The mss. is still too prolix. It needs to be condensed. There is more writing than subject; you see, I read it again last night. A child's loneliness is not enough for a subject. The loneliness should be a catalyst, which does something to the rage of the universal passions of the human heart, the adult world, of which it—the child—is only an observer yet. You dont want to write just "charming" things. Or at least I dont seem to intend to let you.[3]

The point, sir, is that these artists, these masters, address those who may be starting their apprenticeship with a certain concern for the new writer's dignity, and a respect for the art.

John Steinbeck was clever enough (and generous enough) to offer a set of guidelines:

1. Abandon the idea that you are ever going to finish. . . . Write just one page for each day, it helps. Then when it gets finished, you are always surprised.

2. Write freely and as rapidly as possible and throw the whole thing on paper. Never correct or rewrite until the whole thing is down. Rewrite in process is usually found to be an excuse for not going on. It also interferes with flow

---

[3]William Faulkner to Joan Williams, 1952. Reprinted with the permission of Jill Faulkner Summers.

and rhythm which can only come from a kind of unconscious association with the material.

3. Forget your generalized audience. In the first place, the nameless, faceless audience will scare you to death and in the second place, unlike the theatre, it doesn't exist. I have found that sometimes it helps to pick out one person—a real person you know, or an imagined person—and write to that one.

4. If a scene or a section gets the better of you and you still think you want it—bypass it and go on. When you have finished the whole you can come back to it and then you may find that the reason it gave trouble is because it didn't belong there.

5. Beware of a scene that becomes too dear to you, dearer than the rest. . . .

6. If you are using dialogue—say it aloud as you write it. Only then will it have the sound of speech.[4]

Or have a look, sir, at the chain of care and attention with which this book concludes but which is truly at its heart: Caroline Gordon teaches Flannery O'Connor about her own novel, *Wise Blood;* O'Connor is sisterly toward her colleague John Hawkes, who teaches Joanna Scott about clarity; Scott, thirteen years later, passes the favor along. I think of that chain of instruction and support as a complex molecule in the body of our literature, a living part of our literature, an example of caring *for* as well as caring *about*.

I love the work of Dickens, and I wanted him in this book,

---

[4]John Steinbeck to Robert Wallsten, February 13–14, 1962, in *Steinbeck: A Life in Letters,* ed. Elaine A. Steinbeck and Robert Wallsten (New York: Viking, 1975).

yet I found, in the ten Pilgrim Edition volumes of his letters, few enough that encouraged writers to do more than permit him to edit them in either of his magazines, and only one or two—and those so radiant with synthetic, obligatory charm that they gave the pages a greenish glow—which one might call truly encouraging. Joyce's letters were about his great projects, not those of other writers. Hemingway's were, more and more, about advancing and protecting himself. Flaubert, who seems to have known everything about creating prose, spoke mostly of his own.

In our time, however, when so many writers teach or have taught, they are used to apprentices, and they are used to giving them a hand. They know, of course, that one learns to write through long, painful, individual experience. But they are willing to help their students or friends or colleagues find some shortcuts. And they seem to need to say aloud some of the harrowing truths about doing this work. Note how in their letters they do not merely castigate or applaud: they try to honestly instruct. That is why I have included the very specific, detailed letter from John Gardner to the novelist Joanna Higgins: it is alive with Gardner's concern to educate a writer. He was one of our most important teachers of writing, a colleague of Nicholas Delbanco at Bennington (who now continues the tradition at Michigan) and truly appreciated by Raymond Carver, whose own warm, strong letter, included here, will explain to those who did not know him why he is still, actively, missed. In the wonderful letter by Tobias Wolff, we witness some discipline meted out while its rigor is softened by Wolff's real concern for the success of his student, and his genuine affection for the fellow who is not measuring up. Ray Bradbury suggests the absolutely unacademic route: he warns the novelist Dan Chaon, then a seventeen-year-old writer of science fiction, to beware what attending a college might do to his prose. (Mr. Chaon now instructs in a university.) Andre Dubus takes us into the difficult and frighteningly clear realm of morality in writing. David Bradley, Rosellen Brown, Ann Beattie, and Joyce Carol Oates suggest ways to lead the writing life, tactics for surviving the talent that will not let a writer rest, considerations about selfishness (essential and destructive in equal force) and generosities of the spirit. Like Pam Durban or Richard Bausch or George Garrett or James Welch, or any of the other writers in this book, they extend a mentor's hand.

This is a book, sir, of counsel and sustenance. I hope it is an antidote to letters such as yours, which come to men and women in the writing trade each day. You told me the truth, I think, or anyway what passed, between an 11:59 telephone call and your luncheon date that day, for truth. You slugged me around a little, and I guess you didn't much care and, well, *c'est la vie littéraire* and of course you're right.

The writers in this book offer their language to members of the eccentric extended family of fiction writers who—some will even admit it—don't always mind seeing another writer roasted in a surly or careless review, and who are, let us say, attentive to one another's awards, contracts, advances, publicity tours, feature-page interviews and, of course, sales. They know, as Robert Nye does, as do those who have contributed letters to this collection, that writing well usually requires a long, painful apprenticeship. What is so good about the authors of these letters is that they surmount the self, which is our resource and our enemy, and they offer strategy, courage, good will.

Frederick Busch

The readers of this book are about to receive the wisdom of those who know, from the inside of the process, what a writer might need, from time to time, to hear. While you and I, sir, now, at last, conclude our correspondence of thirty years.

Sincerely,
Frederick Busch

Lee K. Abbott

Lee K. Abbott is the author of six collections of short stories, most recently *Living after Midnight* and *Wet Places at Noon*. His work has appeared in *Harper's,* the *Atlantic Monthly*, and *The Georgia Review,* as well as in *The Best American Short Stories* and *The Prize Stories: The O. Henry Awards*. He is the Director of the M.F.A. Program in Creative Writing at the Ohio State University, Columbus.

Fear, trembling, and secret delight: A distinguished short-story writer learns that his son wishes to follow him into the profession.

Speaking for Myself

Dear Kelly,

So, son, at twenty-three you've decided you want to be, Lord love a duck, a writer, yet another master of what Fred calls the "willed word." Oh, man. Truth to tell, I feel more than a little crosswise about this—a whole lot, in fact, like what my father, your long dead and gone grandfather, must've felt the afternoon he all but split my hard head open with the understanding of what such an ambition can, or ought to, be.

You remember the story, right? I wrote about it once in "The True Story of Why I Do What I Do," an essay as bass-ackwards and topside down as this letter is likely to strike you. The shorter version—which, owing to time and disposition, is all I seem capable of today—is this: once upon a time (which, happily, is the way all the best stories start, at least the ones we survive), Gramps was in his cups, semi-blotto on the Cuba Libres he preferred. I was sixteen, maybe fifteen, but I was—drum roll, Ringo—nonetheless a writer. A frigging artiste: moody as a cat, self-absorbed, arrogant, wise with youth, an obvious pain in the keister to all, stranger and not, whose paths I crossed.

I don't know where Mark, your uncle, was that afternoon. Maybe at the Country Club, probably swimming. Me, I was in my bedroom, making up the stuff that only a boy too full of *Playboy* and Blackbeard the Pirate and William Faulkner can make up. At some point, Gramps was in my doorway, his eyes fixed upon me the way he always fixed them upon the animal, mineral or vegetable that had disappointed him. He had a titanic temper, you may remember. The world was broken, its upside sadly down, and he, because everybody else refused to do so, took the insult personally. Corruption, venery, want, deprivation, cheats and scolds, liars and double-dealers, the U.S. Army, golf—Christ on a crutch, he had much to rage about.

"Come with me," he said.

You didn't say "no" to Gramps. You didn't beg to differ. You didn't quibble, as you and your brother are wont to do, or split hairs. You didn't debate, argue, contradict. Instead, when he said "jump," you said "how high?" So I, dutiful and smart, went.

We ended up in the bigger of the two utility rooms at the end of the carport. The day was hot, as are all summer days in southern New Mexico. The room was like an oven on broil, close with the smells of oil and grass clippings and gasoline and dust. We had stopped by the refrigerator on the way out, more ice for his cocktail, and for a moment, while we stood almost elbow to elbow in that room, I imagined myself, oh, ten feet above the pair of us, watching that man sip and savor, watching that gangly boy steel himself against another of the big booms life was already so noisy with.

Gramps, you should know, saved everything: napkins from nightclubs in Havana, pictures of occasions great and small, the novelty gallon of Johnny Walker Red for his hole-in-one, the track shoe charm he got for pole-vaulting cross-handed at Hebron Academy. It was all there, I was to find out shortly, in the steamer trunks and footlockers stacked to the ceiling against the far wall. Oh, geez, the stuff that was to come pouring out. The documents, the letters, the trinkets. Granny had been institutionalized for four or five years, I think, but he hadn't rid himself of her stuff either. The dress she'd worn for their wedding in Harligen, Texas while he was at gunnery school. The blanket I'd had as a baby in Panama. An album of photographs from their first trip to White Sands, the horizon bleached, the sky a wilderness of spookiest blue. All of it a record, if you will, of a small, sad clan doomed to much to and fro. The keepsakes and mementos that tell you where you've been and, by determination and luck, how you got here.

"Here," he said at last, "hold this."

I took his drink, its rum not the only thing in the room to lighten your head or burden your heart, and he went forward, surprisingly nimble for a man in his late fifties. Leapt over the lawnmower, shoved aside the gas can, pitched a rake and a hoe into the far corner. Then he went at those trunks, angry and deliberate both. Something had offended him, that was clear. Then, like a blow below the belt, I understood. It was me, his namesake. I'd flat out pissed him off.

"So you want to be a writer," he said.

From his lips, the word sounded foreign—Zulu or Hindi or Martian—a word big with pain and with terror, but I didn't move. A part of me—the neediest, I'm guessing; the bravest, I'm hoping—understood that I was going to learn something in these minutes, something peculiar and significant and dire as a night on the moon.

And, son, I did.

It took him only minutes to pull down those trunks and footlockers, one tumbling behind him as he yanked another overhead. They crashed and banged, a couple popping open, inside nothing less than the insides of a dozen lives—the dreams and the fears, the hoopla and the horror, the detritus of Uncle Inches and Pay and Aunt Rosalie and his drowned sister Shirley and his dead brother Gideon and his drunk wife Elaine. The last of the things, the first. And me, I was in there, too. Report cards and a report from the school psychologist from the time I'd gone hysterically blind.

"Write it all down," he was saying, over and over, the clatter and clang no more to him than is the Persian our enemies nowadays speak. "Write it all goddam down."

The only line, Kelly, I remember from that essay this is the second telling of is this: In 1963, my father, drunk on Ron Rico and history, was taking seriously, in a way I hadn't or couldn't yet, what it means to be a writer—that ours is an obligation, maybe like that the saints have, to make sense of what, singly or as a tribe, has befallen us; that we, those with the language and the imagination and the memory, must bring shape and order to all that's locked away; that we, yeah, must write it all goddam down—all that bedevils and beleaguers, all that mystifies and frightens, all that's revealed, literally and figuratively, when the "past" is sprung open before us.

Okay, I'm waxing again, right? Preaching, actually. Which, interestingly, is what, over the years, a lot of my students like me to do. They like me to pound the seminar table, to rant, to rail, to get up on my high horse, to hie to the high road and from it, like my father, wag my finger self-righteously at the dickweeds and dingleberries who, Lord in heaven, just aren't working hard enough between their margins, or between their ears. Still, you, like me umpteen umpteens before, asked for it, didn't you?

Me, I never set out to be a writer, at least not the way others have set out to be a doctor or a lawyer or an engineer. No, I just wrote, one goofy yarn after another. Tales of swashbuckling and derring-do. Nick o' time escapes. My first book? A re-telling of *Sir Gawain and the Green Knight*. Illustrated the darn thing, too. Stick figure drawings, sure, but Mrs. Chew, in the 10th grade (British Literature—William Makepeace

Thackeray, Geoffrey Chaucer, Mr. Samuel Taylor Coleridge, the whole dead race of them) let me, over three glorious days, read it to the class. Talk about validation, about the stamp of approval that says—to any who'll listen, albeit—that writing is as fine an endeavor to undertake as is, oh, the building of bridges and the suing of neighbors. Maybe as necessary, too. Certainly, in my narrow view and speaking only for myself, as essential to us and ours as any miracle that drips out of a glass pipet.

Which brings me, given the curious (il)logic I am a victim of, to my second point (expressed in purest Clintonese): it's the work, stupid. Bear with me a moment, okay? I am, as I am in all matters desperate and divine, about to belabor the obvious. My friend Bob Olmstead is fond of saying that we should be in the business of writing the story we can't. An interesting turn of phrase, no? And one, frankly, that's much preoccupied me since I heard it from the back of the canoe during a float Bob and I took one summer down the Juniata River in Pennsylvania. To be sure, his remark has something to do with artistic ambition—the desire, pointed as lust itself, to be story by story, if not page by page, better; to take and pass every test offered by the imagination; to experiment and to risk; to charge around all the corners, personal and aesthetic, you find yourself typing toward. I also think—and here I'm doubtlessly all alone in the canoe—that Bob's observation has much to do with subjecting your work to the stiffest of critical measures, an exercise difficult and betimes troubling to undertake.

Feelings? Well, son, you can't afford to have them. Not about the stuff—the poem, the play, the story, the novel—you mean one day to share with a largely indifferent and always impatient citizenry. In short, yours must be work both meet and felicitous, as finely and carefully wrought as crewel. Yes, you have talent (but, then again, lots of folks have talent, don't they?); in addition, however, you must have the habits of character that are grit and perseverance and a thick skin and intelligence and self-discipline and no little courage. Indeed, you must have a command of the skills, the skills and techniques without which the magic cannot be made (remember, please, what William Gass says: that finding out fiction is made out of words is like finding out that your wife is made out of rubber). But, golly, you may not have feelings. You dare not, on pain of a punishment terrible and everlasting, feel too tender toward or too proud of your work. If art is the result of choices, conscious and not, we make, then make only those choices, line by line by line, that serve the tale, not the teller. You, except as a son and a yellow dog Democrat, aren't important; only the story is.

Tough, huh? Like too many on the planet, you've probably never heard of the poet Robert Francis. Well, Mr. Francis once argued, only half-seriously albeit, that writing—publishing, actually—ought to be a little bit illegal, that the writer ought to pay a fine for presuming to publish. Ten bucks a page, say. You've got a twenty page story, buster? That's two hundred of the dollars you probably don't have right now in your pocket. Quite a proposal, huh? A way, at a minimum, to keep the dilettantes and the tiresome wanna-be's out of the business. Still, it's one I believe vital to be mindful of. So, Kelly, are you willing to do the "time" for your "crime"? Are you willing to say that because the work is good enough, you're eager to pay the piper? Is the work worth the beer money, the movie money, the gas money, the rent?

An instructive anecdote: back in graduate school—this was '75 or '76—I wrote a story for my mentor, Bill Harrison. It was, I see now, a stinker (a third degree felony, say). It was, frankly, a hoot—California breaking off and falling into the ocean—written in an era when hoots, particularly those pouring out of the pens of Barthelme and Coover and Cortázar, seemed to be the only fictions the literate had an appetite for. Still, I was tickled, unreasonably so. I'd gotten off some great lines, phrases wound so tightly they threatened to spring up and poke you in the eye, a vocabulary Latinate enough to get the Pope grinning, its THEME about as subtle as a pair of Halloween wax lips, metaphors savvy enough to be underlined. In the words of my pal Phil Treon? Tits on a ten point. Yeah, the thing was great—stylish enough, I prayed, to put your dad between the covers of *Esquire,* if not the *New Yorker.* Your old man, son, was going to be a star.

So I showed it to Bill. He, as the Cajun comic Justin Wilson used to put it, cast his eye upon it. He smiled, his gold tooth twinkling. "Not yet," he said and hastened me back to the typewriter (yeah, the dark ages before Spell Check and all else got from the lower case god that is Bill Gates). Again, I sat before the thing. It was like waiting for a dog to sing doo-wop. I scratched my head, smoked another pack. "Okay," I told myself. "Maybe not the *New Yorker.* Maybe *Anteaus.*" Time, I have to tell you, was taking its not-so-sweet time. Then—Voila!—an insight (but one only as sharp, it would take me a while yet to find out, as the crease on the pants of a five dollar suit): a fillip there, a tweak here, more froufrou throughout, and, Mr. and Mrs. America, you've got yourselves another winner of the frigging Nobel Prize.

A week later, Bill was casting his eye upon it anew. But no tooth-twinkle this day. "Again," he said, and I, flummoxed and full of feelings, staggered back to the typewriter. I was smart, I told myself. I was able. I was, Praise Jesus, talented.

So why wasn't this thing working? Why hadn't my mentor done a backflip over his desk and immediately dispatched my story to his high-dollar contacts in New Yawk City, the publishing capital of the country? This do-si-do went on for a month, no lie. Me, it, and Bill. More frustration, more drafts, more sly instruction. *The Weekly Reader,* I started thinking. Maybe *Boy's Life.* And then, on yet another afternoon with too much light in it and in the presence of yet another man who commanded my complete attention, I understood (you may picture a lamp—a kleig in this case—going off overhead): though without the props that are trunks and booze, Bill was showing me how silly and perishable and merely crafty the story had been; how, among other sins I'd committed, I had sacrificed character to gimmick; how I'd put style ahead of substance; how I'd indulged in the cheap grab-ass humor of a sophomore; how I'd served up, in Terry Southern's memorable phrase, naught but flash and filigree.

Man, what a moment—to know the difference, as Twain says about diction, between lightning and lightning bug. Me, I had been wrought up about which tab fit into which slot—story, alas, as contraption. But Bill, arch as a matinee villain, had been concerned that I learn what the writing was for—that LKA, thereafter and evermore, would never again write a story that cost him only time to get into English.

Yeah, Kelly, it's the story you can't, the one you'll wave under St. Peter's nose when the hour comes to exit this vale of etceteras.

Over a thousand words ago, I'd meant to be inspirational, son. Honest Injun. I'd meant to tell you, never mind the hugger-mugger of this prose, that writing, when it's going well, is

better than sex; that many delights, unbidden and unpredictable, await on, say, page five or page fifty; that nothing
stirs the gut more than a sentence that bends time toward
beauty; that the voices you're to hear will be both scary and
irresistible; that, effort by effort, you will improve; that the
world, parlous and inchoate and peculiar and difficult, will
nonetheless yield up its secrets; that you will be poleaxed by
something you didn't know you knew; that, ironically and
necessarily, you will not be satisfied with anything you produce; that, as Gertrude Stein said, you will become only older
and different.

But I'm tired now. Another long day here in our shitkicker
paradise. Another day with too much heart in it, too much
brain. Another day when the keyboard, every ugly button of
it, has let me down. I want to hit a bucket of balls, son. That's
all—just me, the driving range, the lob wedge, high heaven,
and only a backswing to fret about. Another "art" to perfect.
I have, in the words of John Clellon Holmes, nothing more to
declare. Except this: imagine you're here, on the deck, night-
time coming on hard from the east. Mom's gone down the
valley—at Becky's, say, quilting. It's just you and me and Al
the Wonderdog. I've got my Redeye, you your bottle of Bud.
You're back from Sweden or Wales or Ohio, wherever the
dickens you were last. I'm back from another trip to fatten
the checkbook, me another hour nearer my last.

I've been talking the talk, son. Railing against the cowards
and cry-babies who've ransacked the ivory tower. The harri-
dans and the epicenes, the petty tyrants and the tin pot ide-
ologues. Don't write drunk, I've told you. Or stoned. Get a
reader, I've told you. Better yet, be a reader. Write fan letters.
Show up for readings and the like. Fret not about fame and
fortune. Take every opportunity to write well. Rewrite.

Rewrite again. Pay your bills promptly. Say "please" and "thank you." Change your oil every three thousand miles.

Ah, it's late, isn't it, dreamland the only place left to go? So, this: write it all down, Kelly. The spit and string and sweat of us, the purl and sweep of our condemned kind. Write it all down. The hopes and fears we are, the yip and yike we are in the dark. The hand and head and heart of us. Write it all down.

Write it all goddam down.

Richard Bausch

Richard Bausch is the author of eight novels and four collections of stories, including the novels *Rebel Powers, Violence,* and *Good Evening Mr. & Mrs. America and All the Ships at Sea,* and the story collections *The Fireman's Wife, Rare & Endangered Species,* and *Selected Stories* (Modern Library). His novel *The Last Good Time* was made into a motion picture. He has won two National Magazine Awards, a National Endowment for the Arts Fellowship, a Guggenheim Fellowship, the Lila Wallace Reader's Digest Fund Writer's Award, and the Award of the American Academy of Arts and Letters. His most recent novel, *In the Night Season,* appeared in spring 1998. He is Heritage Professor of Writing at George Mason University and lives in rural Virginia with his wife, Karen, and their five children.

Ten commandments about the art and craft from a writer who is a true believer in the virtues of the profession.

Dear Writer

Dear Writer,

While there are of course thousands of reasons why people begin to write—some of them rather shabby ones, too—there usually is only one reason why they continue: and that is that the work has become necessary. We are habit forming creatures, and this work is very habit forming if one has any talent at all. Of course, you don't know when you begin if you really *have* any talent. You hope you do; perhaps you even suspect that you do. Sometimes you go back and forth, believing on some days, and disbelieving on others. Mostly you believe the last thing you read or heard concerning the work, and you probably tend to listen to the negative things more; the last negative thing you heard has sunk deeper into you and has lasted a longer time than any positive comment; painful as this is, it is also perfectly normal.

My best advice has nothing to do with technique, or aesthetics or the craft itself, really. It is more to do with training one's self to be shrewd. To live intelligently where the work is concerned: as I have said many times in classes, writing is not an indulgence; the indulgences are what you give up to write. You don't go to as many parties, you don't watch as much television (I don't watch it at all, anymore), you don't listen to as much music. You make decisions in light of what you have to do in a given day, and everything *except* the life you lead with your family is subordinated to the hours you must work. How much you get done depends in large part not on your talent—which is whatever it is, and is mostly constant—but on your own attitude *about* what you are doing.

So.

I have devised a sort of Ten Commandments for you, that are

the result of some of my own struggles with this blessed occupation, and of what I have been able to learn from reading or being around writers who are better than I. Here they are.

1. Read.

You must try to know everything that has ever been written that is worth remembering, and you must keep up with what your contemporaries are doing. Fitzgerald's advice to his daughter, Scottie, is as good as any there is on this subject: you must try to *absorb* (italics mine) six good authors a year. This means that you do not read books as an English Major is trained to read them; you *swallow* them. You *ingest* them, and move on. You do not stop to analyze or think much; you just take them into yourself, and go on to the next one. And you read obsessively, too: if you really like something, you read it over and over through the years. You come to know the world's literature by heart. Every good writer I know or have known began with an insatiable appetite for books, for plundering what is in them, for the nourishment provided by them, that you can't get from any other source.

2. Imitate.

While you are doing this reading, you spend time trying to sound like the various authors—just as a painter, learning to paint, sets up his easel in the museum and *copies* the work of the masters. You learn by trying the sound and the stance of other writers. You develop an ear, through your reading and imitating, for how good writing is *supposed* to sound.

3. "Be regular and ordinary in your habits, like a Petit Bourgeois, so you may be violent and original in your work."

This comes from Flaubert, and is quite good advice. It has

to do with what I was talking about in the first paragraph, and is of course better expressed. The thing that separates the amateur writer from the professional, often enough, is simply the amount of time spent working the craft. Know that if you really want to write, if you hope to produce something that will stand up to the winds of criticism and the scrutiny of strangers, you are going to have to work harder than you ever worked on anything else in your life—hour upon hour upon hour, with nothing in the way of encouragement, no good feeling except the sense that you have been true to the silently admonishing example of the writers who came before you, the ones whose company you would like to be in, and of whose respect you would like to be worthy.

4. Train yourself to be able to work anywhere.

Once, when our first child was a baby, my mother came to visit, and after the baby went to sleep I began tiptoeing around trying to make no noise. My mother said, "What the heck are you doing?" I said, "The Baby's asleep." She said, "Have some friends over, put some music on, rattle some dishes, make noise. You're training that boy to be a bad sleeper." That wise advice applies to this craft, too. If you set up a certain area of expectation about when and how you'll be able to do the work, you train yourself to be silent. Shostakovitch wrote his famous 7th Symphony, the Leningrad Symphony, *during* the siege of Leningrad. Bombs were falling all around him, and he understood perfectly well that there was a very good chance he would die within the next few hours, or days. Teach yourself to write in busy places, under the barrage of noises the world makes—work in rooms where children are playing, with music on, even with the television on. Work in the faith that if something is really good, it will not escape back into oblivion if you get distracted from it. It will turn up again. There is no known excuse for not working, *when you are supposed to be working.* Remember that it is an absurdity to put writing *before* the life you have to lead—and I'm not talking about leisure. I'm talking about the responsibility you have to the people you love, and who love you back—no arduousness in the craft or art should ever occupy one second of the time you are supposed to be spending with your family. It has never been a question of the one or the other, and writers who say it is are lying to themselves, are providing an excuse to be bad people. They are thinking of writing as a pretext for bad behavior. It has never been anything of the sort.

5. Be patient.

You are trying to do something that is harder than just about anything there is to do, even when it feels easy. You will write many more failures than successes. Say to yourself, *I accept failure as the condition of this life, this work. I freely accept it as my destiny.* Then go on and do the work. You never ask yourself anything beyond *did I work today?*

6. Be Willing.

Accepting failure as a part of your destiny, learn to be willing to fail, to take the chances that often lead to failure, in the hope that one of them might lead to something good. *Be open for business,* all the time. You must try to be that person on whom nothing is lost. This does not mean that you are taking notes while people around you suffer. You are not that kind of observer. It means that *in the work room* you are willing to follow whatever your dreaming presents you with, openly and without judgment or attitude or even opinions.

7. Eschew politics.

If you have opinions, leave them out of the workplace. If you have anything worthwhile to say, let it surprise you. John Gardner once told me, "If one of your characters makes a long speech filled with his deepest held beliefs, make sure *you* don't believe one word of it." I think that is very sound advice. You are in the business of portraying the personal life, the personal cost of events, so even if history is part of your story, it should only serve as backdrop. The writers who have gotten into trouble with despots over the shameful history of tyranny did so because they insisted on *not paying any attention to the politics* except as it applied to the personal lives of the people they were creating. They told the truth, in other words, and refused to *be* political. The paradoxical truth of the matter is that a writer who pays attention to the personal life is subversive precisely because he refuses to pay attention to anything else. Bad politics hurts people on the personal level and good writers report from there about the damage. And the totalitarians are rightfully afraid of those writers.

8. Do not think, dream.

If you believe you are thinking when you write, make yourself *stop* thinking. You are trying to tap a part of yourself that is closest to the dreaming side, the side that is most active when you sleep. You are trying to recover the literal vision of a child. This is what Flannery O'Connor means when she says "a good story is literal in the same sense that a child's drawing is literal." Dream the story up, make it up, be fanciful, follow what occurs to you to say, and try not to worry about whether or not it's smart, or shows your sensitive nature in the best light, or delivers the matters of living that you think you have learned. Just dream it up and let the thing play itself out as it seems to want to, and then write it again, and still again, dreaming it through, and *then* try to be terribly smart about it. Read it with the cold detachment of a doctor looking at an x ray. Which is to say that you must learn to re-read your own sentences as a stranger might. And say everything aloud. Listen to how it *sounds.*

9. Don't compare yourself to anyone, and learn to keep from building expectations.

People develop at different rates, with different results, and luck is also involved. Your only worry for yourself should be *did I work today?* Be happy for the successes of your friends, because good fortune for one of us is good fortune for all of us. When a friend or acquaintance has good luck, you may feel envy because envy is a natural human reaction; but, as George Garrett once put it, when that stuff rises to your mind, you must train yourself to *contend* with it there. That is what determines everything else about you as an artist. You will never write anything worth keeping if you allow yourself to give in to petty worries over whether you are treated as you think you deserve, or your rewards are commensurate to the work you've done. That will almost never be the case, and the artist who expects great rewards and complete understanding is a fool.

10. Be wary of all general advice.

Discard everything that precedes this commandment if, for you, it gets in the way of writing good stories. Because for every last assertion in this letter, there are several notable exceptions.

Finally, try to remember that what you are aiming to do is a beautiful—even a noble—thing, trying to write, or make, the truth as straightly and honestly and artfully as you can; and that it is also, always, an inherently optimistic act, because it stems from the belief that there will be civilized others whose sensibilities you may affect, if you are lucky and good and faithful to the task at hand. No matter how tragic the vision, it is always a hopeful occupation, and therefore you have to cultivate your ability to balance things: to entertain high hopes without allowing those hopes to become expectations. To do your work without worrying too much about what the world will have to say about it, or do to it. Mostly, of course, the world will ignore it, and so you will have that in common with many very great writers, good men and women who came before you. By giving it everything you have, and being faithful to the work, you honor their fidelity to it; you *partake* of it, you accept their silent admonition to write like all hell, to be as good as they were.

Richard Bausch

Charles Baxter

Charles Baxter is the author of two novels (*First Light* and *Shadow Play*) and four books of stories, the most recent of which is *Believers*. He is also the author of a book of essays on fiction, *Burning Down the House*. His fiction has been widely anthologized. He lives in Ann Arbor and teaches at the University of Michigan.

A meditation on fiction writing and fiction writers becomes, as well, a bit of a trompe l'oeil *and an example of how to make fiction.*

Full of It

Dear ———,

I am writing this letter to you from a cabin north of Duluth, Minnesota, on Lake Superior. On my left are high windows that face southeast, toward the ledge rock down by the water. I'm typing this letter at the dining room table, and I've positioned myself so that I can gaze out through the windows on the west side of the room. I can see several poplars, a stand of scrubby pines, and, between them and me, the snow that's been falling most of the morning. In the distance I can hear waves breaking on the rocks, and from inside the house, the sound of the water heater clicking on and off. It's still and peaceful here, a quietness and peacefulness that many would-be writers associate with writing and creative activity.

Believe me, it has not always been this way. Writing, in my case, began with exhilaration, misery, and furor.

This time around, I had to travel a day-and-a-half to get to this place, and I lost a pair of reading glasses along the way. I left them behind on the train. Being farsighted, I can't at this moment see clearly the words that I am writing and that are displayed on the laptop. They're almost completely blurred. I'm not even *trying* to read them. Instead, I am watching the pines and the snow while I type. It's a kind of daydreaming, soul-satisfying and extremely pleasant, like having the gift to be able to write music without having to hear it, except internally.

When I told a friend that I planned to come up here—to this cabin, on the lake, near the woods—for four days just to write, she said, with a pleasant laugh, "That's great. I envy you."

I had to think about this. I don't find it curious that some people should envy writers, but for the most part I think that people don't actually envy them very much (when they think about writers at all), and they probably envy them less now than they used to a few decades ago. People who have to do difficult or meaningless work often envy, with good reason, the life of the artist. Such a life can appear to be fulfilling and, in its way, luxurious. It can also look suspiciously like an escape from base-line realities. As a compensating punishment, outsiders like to imagine the artist being plagued by poverty and unworldliness, which of course is what artists often have, and get.

Young musicians still starve, fledgling painters starve, writers starve. Well, they don't starve, but they don't always eat well or buy Porsches, and the idea that they're being self-indulgent is a common accusation, leveled against the would-be artist by friends, lovers, spouses, and family members. You don't often hear investment bankers being accused of self-indulgence, although, as a group, they are, at least in recent reports of their behavior, noteworthy for that quality, but their indulgences sometimes make money, thereby exonerating them. The artist who fails, furthermore, has not beaten the odds, because the odds always favor failure and frequently justify the predictions. Fiction writers may have a gift, but they also have an affliction, and this affliction is not often noticed and not much discussed. You need to know about it, and I'll try to describe it, but I have to go out of my way to apologize first.

My trouble is that I don't really believe in most wisdom: not in this letter to you, not my own wisdom, not anybody's. As you must know by now, most "wisdom" is not wisdom. It's pernicious attitudinizing bullshit. Too often, what passes for wisdom is simply somebody's personal prejudice masquerading as truth. It's ideological poison seeking an object. With good reason, young people often distrust wisdom from the old. They see the coerciveness it usually masks, the effort to justify past mistakes by replicating them in the young. Lars Gustafsson: "We take steps to justify the steps we have already taken . . . stubbornly, we stay on in the bad hotel to justify the fact that we were once stupid enough to check in there."

Most young people can't get away from this scene of the self-justification of error fast enough. True wisdom is somewhat private, while public wisdom tends to be wheezing and arcane and irrelevant, and most of the time there's no love in its dissemination. Wisdom from the middle-aged and the old has a tendency nearly always to miss its mark, to strike the wrong tone (usually one of smug self-importance) and to become fatuous. The fraudulently wise, the stupidly sermoniacal, are, on stage, figures of comedy and menace, like Polonius. Audiences of *Hamlet* are often pleased to see Polonius get what they think he deserves—a knife in the heart.

That's why I'm having trouble writing to you. It's a problem in tone. I keep starting this letter and throwing it away (though, without my reading glasses, I can't find the trash icon). I think you should make your own mistakes, the way that I made mine. Why should you try to avoid failure, misery, heartbreak, sorrow, drunkenness, sexual confusion and apathy? I couldn't avoid them, you probably won't, and they will end up serving as resources for your writing. I managed to live through them, though I expect to see those bad friends again, some day.

I myself was both arrogant and insecure as a young writer;

I think I must have been insufferable, thanks to my ignorance and knowingness—a dangerous combination, and quite inflammatory, though not all that unusual. Before William Faulkner became the William Faulkner we know, he was of course a young unfamous man, a "writer-about-to-be," to use Walter Abish's wonderful phrase. And what did the people in Faulkner's home town call this young unknown man with great writerly ambitions, who affected to stroll around town with a walking stick, like an aristocrat, or a Count? "Count No-Count," was the name they found for him.

They were the first harbingers of the Fraud Police, who will dog your heels for much of your life. I'll be talking more about those sinister patrolmen later.

Advice is almost as bad as wisdom, especially when it hasn't been asked for. If you've read Rilke's *Letters to a Young Poet,* you'll notice that Rilke takes his young writer-friend very seriously, so seriously, in fact, that Rilke's book achieves a kind of spiritual greatness of an odd sort, as if poetry and genius could be learned from a conduct-manual. At the same time, Rilke's book is almost entirely impractical. It teaches you nothing except how Rilke felt about being a poet. That's enormously important, but useless. Rilke is explaining to an ordinary person with an ambition to be a poet what it's like to be a genius, and he is pretending for appearance's sake that anyone can aspire to genius. Of course anyone can, but it'll wreck your life if you don't have the capacity for it, and it may wreck your life even if you do. But a life, Rilke might have said, may be a small price to pay for great poems. If you can give up your life for your country, why shouldn't you give it up for poetry? It's like a saint explaining to a house painter the steps to becoming a saint. It's not that the saint is wrong. He is, after all, a saint. (Rilke, after all, is Rilke.) The real problem is that only Rilke could be Rilke. Others have tried to be him, and naturally have failed. They can, big surprise, only succeed at being themselves.

Rilke's seemingly implicit promise—"See: you can do what I do, be what I am"—tends to become an obsession when planted in others. Those who have suffered that particular obsession have felt their lives dwindling. The only relief from an obsession is to be divested of it, not to indulge it. The curse that The Great (like Rilke) leave behind is the curse of their absolutely unfollowable example. Their lives and their work cannot be replicated and they create a bizarre perspective when they seek to offer advice.

The shadow Rilke casts is great and, as he must have hoped, absolute. The wings of his spirit can enfold both the knowing and the innocent who wander too close to him. They can suffocate anyone who tries to take his advice, to follow his example.

The problem is this: Rilke, like many other European artists of the early part of the twentieth century, thought of poetry as a calling, and of art generally as a spiritual project that contained within it a core of redemption and redemptive force, though his poetry is never scrupulously clear about what form this redemption would actually take. Still, his message is straightforward: Poetry can save you. *You must change your life.* Americans, who are at heart pragmatic, have rarely believed that art can solve much of anything or redeem anyone. If you tell them, "Poetry can save you," they are likely to say, "From what?" But they do like to buy how-to books, and, in a general way, they like to be told how to do something. Because fiction is even less transcendent than poetry is, and is more remunerative, Americans, at least, seem to respect it, or used to. There are many how-to-write manuals on the bookstore shelves, most of them quite un-Rilkean and extremely practical. All the same, for fifty years, few people have seriously thought that the writing or reading of fiction is a sacred activity, or even much of an occupation, using the conventional yardsticks.

Nevertheless: here I am in this quiet house. I don't care if I am in a minority. I am writing these words to you, watching the snow fall, happy to think of myself as a writer, someone who has found a calling, and wondering: What can I say that will be of any use?

The first and last thing to say is, "I am happy, despite all my failures." And more: *I am almost unbelievably lucky.* But the point is not me at all. The point has to do with an art, and a condition.

The condition first.

Probably you are a great or a good noticer. You may well be the one in your family who paid attention to your family members more than the others did. You sometimes knew what they would say before they actually said it. When they were out of the room, their voices sounded in your inner ear. Quite possibly, you were good at imitating all of them. You were the watcher. Sometimes, you felt like a spy: you were spying on the whole of life itself. This condition has its own kind of excitement and pathos, but it very clearly carries along with its discoveries a feeling of tension, and estrangement. Without quite knowing how, you fell just a bit outside the groups of which you were a member.

And if you were like me, you often sat in the back of the class near the window, daydreaming. You could concentrate but in an extremely selective manner. Much of the time, while you were observing the world, you yourself were in a fog. You *were* that fog. You hardly knew who you were. Sometimes you felt like everybody. You may have been very good at telling jokes and stories, keeping the other kids amused or interested for hours, but some part of you watched all this and *watched how others were reacting to you.* I'm not very good at telling jokes, but I do like to tell stories, and sometimes, in school, when I did so, my friends would say, "Baxter, you're full of it."

I was. I am.

Writers also have an early tendency toward funny and malicious gossip, but in this they are not particularly different from much of anyone else.

It's in the later years of adolescence that writers, as a group, begin to feel a particular affliction, which is also a gift. . . . This feeling, which I think is peculiar to writers and more specifically to fiction writers, is that of feeling as if you are carrying a whole landscape of people around inside you. In one of Pynchon's novels this condition is described as "coming on like a whole roomful of people." You may not know who you are (my first book was titled *Chameleon*), but you often do know who these internalized people are, whose tantalizing stories are beginning to press out on you like something growing from the inside out, something extruded. You are full of it; you are full of them.

You are full of the possibility of characters and narrative.

I have not seen this condition described accurately much of anywhere. Kierkegaard, in *Repetition,* remarks on how quickly and how often young men, after falling in love with a woman, draw back slightly and find themselves becoming addicted to the experience they have just had of falling in love, which requires, not the continuation of love itself, but the repetition of the experience of falling-in-love, thus turning the object of love, the loved one, into a pretext, and the lover into a sort of addict. (Don Juan is an addict.) A sign of this, Kierkegaard says, is writing—usually love poems. Writers of fiction are a bit like that. They have fallen *into* the characters whom they have observed and imagined and loved. And the only way to get out of that feeling is to tell the story of that character. But it's not enough to tell one story. Because there are so many characters buried within the self, the only sensible activity is, to use Gertrude Stein's phrase, "telling it again and again." There is something in this process that resembles the dynamics of addiction. The practice of most arts is very hard to give up once you've started, and few people ever manage to stop doing it.

The young fiction writer—you—carries a burden of sorts. You are lugging something around that seems to be part of your being, or, as we would say now, is "hard wired" into you, so much so that you have become its container, but the only way to express it—almost literally, to bring it out—is to write it. What "it" is, in this case, is a piling-up of selves, of beings, and of stories that are being experienced *from the inside*. What is it like to be you, to be me? You can't answer that question by answering it discursively. You can only answer it by telling a story. That's not therapy. You're not sick. You're just a certain kind of human being. It's exactly like the necessity the musician has in humming a tune or playing a piano, or the necessity an artist has in doodling and sketching and drawing and painting. It's almost involuntary. Something needs to get out: Not expressed but *extruded*. As the composer Camille Saint-Saëns remarked, "I write music the way an apple tree produces apples."

You would feel this necessity even if the novel died, even if there were no audience for fiction (but there always will be), even if it seemed that you might never be published. You would feel the press of stories and characters outward from yourself toward the world, no matter what the conditions might be of publication and distribution. Other literature has simply inspired and inflamed you. In Henry James' words, you are "a reader who has been moved to emulation." It's as if you've been given instructions: *Get it all down.* The real question is what to do about it, this gift and affliction, how to organize your life so that the conditions of that life don't shape up as a full-fledged disaster. The size of a life-disaster is often proportional to the size of the ambition. Just because you hear the call doesn't mean that you are saved.

Women and men who have decided to be fiction writers have a certain fanaticism. Sometimes this fanaticism is well con-cealed, but more often it isn't. They—you—need it, to get you through the bad times and the long apprenticeship. Learning any craft alters the conditions of your being. Poets, like math-ematicians, ripen early, but fiction writers tend to take longer to get their world on paper because that world has to be observed in predatory detail and because the subtleties of plot, setting, tone and dialogue are, like the mechanics of brain surgery, so difficult to master. Fanaticism ignores cur-rent conditions (i.e., you are living in a garage, surviving on peanut butter sandwiches, and writing a Great Novel that no one, so far, has read, or wants to) in the hope of some condi-tion that may arrive at a distant point in the future. Fanaticism and dedication and doggedness and stubbornness are your angels. They keep the demon of discouragement at bay. But, given the demands of the craft, it is no wonder that so many of its practitioners—women and men—come out at the other end of the process as drunks, bullies, windbags, bespoke-suited merchants of smarm, and assholes. The wonder is that *any* of them come out as decent human beings. But some do.

A writer's life is tricky to sustain. The debased romanticism that is sometimes associated with it—the sordid glamour of living in an attic, being a drunken oaf or a bully, getting into fistfights à la Bukowski—needs to be discarded, and fast.

I was a late starter, a painfully slow learner. I remember having a great idea for a story while riding a Minneapolis city bus at the age of thirteen. I was on fire with it. The idea was: An inmate of a mental hospital who thinks he is Christ *actually is Christ!* I thought this idea was so good that I was terrified that someone would steal it. I wanted to register this idea in the United States copyright office, though I didn't know how. I kept having ideas like this for years and would walk around in public with a sly, secretive smile on my face.

I first tried to write a novel at the age of twenty-two. I had only taken one creative writing class (insecurity, arrogance), and the single scene of this novel I can remember writing was one in which a man throws himself out of a window of a high-rise building. The man's fall is described in phantasmagoric detail. Everything in my writing was apocalyptic and cataclysmic.

Four years later, armed with an advanced degree and a job, I sat down in my free hours to write my first completed novel, *Ground Zero,* which you will never read because it has never been published and never will be. I think—I hope—no copy of it exists anymore. It was about a world in which *everyone starts lying about everything all the time!* Remember—in my defense—that this was the era of Johnson and Nixon and the war in Vietnam. I wrote this novel in a state of high excitement. I was exhilarated by almost every one of my sentences. I suspected I was a genius but was careful to keep this stupendous secret to myself. Angels and devils, truth and lying, ultimate realities all found their way into this book. A few people read it, most were mystified by it (I was mystified by their mystification—how could they not see how astoundingly good this book was?), and it found its way to a few editors, all of whom said it was interesting but that it was "not for us."

Undeterred, and now, by a set of bizarre circumstances, armed with an agent, I then sat down and for the next two years wrote my second novel, *Media Event,* which you have not read because it has never been published and never will be. It was about . . . oh, never mind. I wrote this book in a state of high excitement—once again, I was exhilarated by my sentences and by my visionary power. I sent it to the agent I had acquired by writing *Ground Zero* and waited for her excited, blubberingly enthusiastic phone call.

I waited and waited. Finally I decided to call her myself. It was a summer afternoon. In Minnesota, my mother was dying of emphysema and heart failure. I was hoping that I might have some good news for her. Here at home, my wife was pregnant, and we were, despite my job, flat broke. I had spent the last five years of my life trying to become a fiction writer, to get a foothold. That afternoon, I was in the bedroom, sitting on the bed, and the sun was shining through the west-facing windows, and I was getting up my courage, steeling it, as people say, to the sticking-point.

After I dialed the agency's number, my agent, Julia, answered. I identified myself, and she said hi. There was a brief pause, an expressive air-pocket of dead silence. I explained to her that a friend, a writer who was a visiting professor at my university, had read my new novel manuscript and had said that it might be snapped up at Alfred A. Knopf, his own publisher. I asked what she thought its chances were there.

"Charlie," she said. "Don't you want to know what I think of your new novel? The one you just sent me?"

"Yes, Julie, of course I do."

There was another pause, and I heard her taking a breath. "I hate it," she said, with what seemed to be an odd satisfaction.

"You *hate* it?" My mouth had turned instantly to cotton.

"Yes, I hate it. Isn't that puzzling? I can't figure it out. How strange. Tell me why I hate it."

"What?"

"Tell me why I hate your novel."

"Julie," I said, trying to hold my head up while the room started to spin, "I have no idea why you hate my novel."

"Of course you do. Oh, sure, you must. *You wrote it.* Tell me why I hate it."

"I don't know," I said.

"Oh, you must. Please. Give it a try. Help me out here. Tell me why I hate your novel. Is it the characters? Is it the plot? I just don't get it. I don't get *any* of it. So," she said, cheerfully, "is that it? The *whole thing?* Is that why I hate your novel?"

That, almost word-for-word, is what she said to me up to that point, but I don't remember the rest of the conversation, except for the news that naturally she no longer wanted to represent me. I went into a sort of shock and can remember nothing else from the rest of the day.

Somewhat deterred by now, but still, after my recovery, brimming with guarded enthusiasm, I subsequently sat down, during those brief moments between child-care and class-preparations, to write my third novel, *In Hibernation,* which you have never read because it was never published . . . etc. Thanks to a new set of bizarre circumstances, I had acquired a different agent. When I finished *In Hibernation,* I gave it to my wife, who seemed unable to finish it. Nevertheless, I bravely sent it to my new agent, who called and told me with great tact and kindness, this time, that no one at the agency thought it was marketable; in other words, they would not be sending it out. I mailed a copy of the manuscript to a literary-minded friend on the West Coast—he's now a book reviewer there—who said to me over the phone a couple of weeks later, "Charlie, maybe your imagination is poisoned right at the source."

The condition into which I fell is one that you may discover for yourself. I believed that I knew what I wanted to do with my life, but I would not be allowed to do it in the way that I had imagined. People seemed to dislike what I produced and could not be persuaded to like it. I carried around within me stories that had, I thought, an aura to them. But these stories struck no chords in anyone else. No one heard the chords, and no one saw the aura. I thought I was reasonably smart. At least: smart enough. And reasonably talented. But none of it was working. I fell down very far into several intellectual and spiritual and emotional abysses, many of them inter-connected. I could draw you a map. I felt as if my nerves had moved out to the surface of my skin; I felt humiliated and exposed. I think that, at this point in my life, only my wife and my child and my job kept me anchored to the world of the living.

I was close to being a menace to myself. I decided, among other resolutions, that I would never write another novel.

I also decided that I would never be a writer, in the sense

in which that word is commonly used. What I thought was my calling probably wasn't my calling after all—that in fact I didn't have a calling except to be a decent human being, a teacher, a husband, and a father, if indeed I could manage that. I was in my early thirties by this time and felt that I had become an expert on failure and the day-to-day management of despair. Much of the time my mouth was full of ashes. I found that I had a new streak of verbal cruelty that I could not always control. I decided to write one last piece, on my particular subject, about a young man who fails to be a good musician and who becomes a critic instead. It was a story called "Harmony of the World," and I sent it to a local quarterly, *Michigan Quarterly Review,* expecting the usual rejection and scathing comments to which I was becoming accustomed.

A few weeks later I was watching TV in the basement when the phone rang. It was the editor of *Michigan Quarterly Review,* Laurence Goldstein. He told me that he had read my story; he was quite enthusiastic about it. And then he asked me a question. I sometimes remind him of this moment, because it struck me then, and strikes me now, as one of the kindest questions anyone has ever asked me, and because it suggested ever so slightly that I might be somebody, rather than the nobody I had constructed for myself and elaborately resigned myself to being.

"Who are you?" he inquired.

He was a stranger, and yet he asked as if the answer might be worth knowing.

For the next five years I wrote about failure. It had become my subject, my koan, my home base, my infinitely renewable resource. The abyss turned into a mineshaft. My first book, a collection of stories titled with nasty irony *Harmony of the World,* appeared in 1984. The book deals with the failure of characters to do successfully what they have set out to do. It's an interesting subject, though slightly un-American. By the time the book appeared, I was thirty-seven. After my sister-in-law read it, she asked me, over cocktails, "Why do you write about characters with such pathetic little lives?"

Because I know them, I said, or wanted to say. Besides, who are your people? These are *my* people. They're *telling.* In the title story, there is a character named Luther Stecker who asks the narrator, a pianist, why his playing makes him— Stecker—sick. *Why,* he asks, *do I hate your playing?* Tell me. Be courageous. Tell me why I hate your playing. (What I, as a writer, was doing in this story might be called "taking my demons out of the unemployment line and putting them to work.") Thank you, Julie, wherever you are, for your cruelty to me. Couldn't have done it without you.

In my next book of stories, called *Through the Safety Net,* there is a story called "Media Event," and another story, called "Gryphon," in which an atmosphere of constant lying is created in a classroom, very much as it was in *Ground Zero,* and there is another story called "The Eleventh Floor," in which remnants of *In Hibernation* are visible. As my aunt used to say, "Nothing is ever gained or lost in the universe," and I suppose I had learned that lesson. *Through the Safety Net* is, in part, a massive salvage operation, in which a few moments are retrieved from my personal sunken scrapheap of failure.

It seems a shame to say so, but the hardest part of being a writer is not the long hours of learning the craft, but learning how to survive the dark nights of the soul. There are many such nights, far too many, as you will discover. I hate to be the one to bring you this news, but someone should.

Part of the deal of having a soul at all includes the requirement that you go through several dark nights. No soul, no dark nights. But when they come, they have a surprisingly creepy power, and almost no one tells you how to deal with them. You can do illegal drugs or take psychoactive pills, you can have affairs or masturbate, you can watch movies 'til dawn, but that only produces what doctors call "symptomatic relief." In these nights you confront your own doubts, lack of self-confidence, the futility of what you are doing, and the various ways in which you fail to measure up. Feelings of inadequacy are the black-lung disease of writing. These are the nights during which the Fraud Police come to knock on your door.

Psychologists have their own name for this set of feelings. (They have clinical names for most of our emotions by now.) They call it "imposter-syndrome." Imposter-syndrome is endemic to the art of writing because gifts—the clear evidence of talent—are not so clearly associated with writing as they are with music and graphic art. Not everyone has perfect pitch, not everyone can carry a tune, not everyone can draw or create an interesting representation of something on canvas. But almost every goddamn moron can write prose.

Furthermore, anyone's apprenticeship in the writing of fiction has several stages, at least one of which involves an imposture. To be a novelist or short story writer, you first have to pretend to be a novelist or a short story writer. By great imaginative daring, you start out as Count No-Count. Everyone does. Everyone starts as a mere scribbler. Proust got his start as a pesky dandified social layabout with no recognizable talents except for making conversation and noticing everybody. So what do *you* do? You sit down and pretend to write a novel by actually trying to write one without knowing how to do it. (It is clearly not a rule-governed activity; there are only rules-of-thumb that sometimes work.) As you pretend to write your novel, you learn, if you're lucky, actually how to do it. You learn this intuitively. After you've learned how to do it, you proceed to write another novel, and, if you're lucky, it turns out to be a real novel.

The trouble is that the first stage—of pretending to be a writer—never quite disappears. And there is, in this art, no ultimate validation, again because it's not a rule-governed activity. The ultimate verdict never comes in. God tends to be silent in matters of art and literary criticism. Reviewers and editors who pretend to be God make fools of themselves. Besides, what's the yardstick? It's hard to make a lot of money from writing, and even if you did make a lot of money, what then? You might be labeled as a hack. No one asked you to do what you're doing, so you can't satisfy that person by doing it. You don't find out until much much later that you may have helped some people who have read your work. Reviews may eventually come, and they're good (or bad), and there are prizes, and you get them (or don't). When one of my novels was published, one reviewer said it was destined to be a classic, and another reviewer—Michael Upchurch (how could I forget?)—said the book was a clear sign of my incompetence as a novelist. Someone is always doing better than you are, someone is always being loved a little more, someone is always telling you that the work is not up to snuff, or that it shows incompetence, or a decline.

Compared to poets, however, you have one lucky break. If you write a novel or a book of short stories, most readers will say, "This novel is good (or bad)." They won't deny that at least you've written a novel. Fiction doesn't seem to have an essence in quite the way that poetry does. Having an essence changes everything. The terrible charge of total inauthenticity in the writing of poetry is commonplace as a result of this business of poetry's having an essence. That's why people are always saying, "That's a real poem," or "That's *not* poetry at all." They're talking about poetry as written material that has some almost indescribable core, a radiant gist. Someone who produces this essence is a poet, or a "real poet." Someone who writes verses but does not produce this essence is called a "poetaster." A poetaster is a fraudulent poet, a non-poet.

Luckily for us, there is no such thing as a prosetaster. No such word, at least in English. Because fiction has no essence, any novel that gets written up one way or another is, almost by default, a real novel.

Still, you can wake up at night and feel like a fraud. That probably happens to you now, before anyone has said your work is any good, and it will continue to happen, once you are published and are reviewed. The fraud-feeling is very mysterious and, for most of us, never quite goes away. Prozac and Xanax are sometimes prescribed to banish it. By contrast, bracing self-confidence among writers is a rare commodity and often a sign of psychic instability.

I recently saw Toni Morrison on national television. It was *Sixty Minutes.* In front of a large audience, she was asked if she thought she was a great writer. She smiled and laughed, then nodded, and said, well, yes, but she had *always* thought that she was a great writer. Her laughter made the admission appear to be part of an outburst of great good humor, even gaiety, that the audience could share, as in an interview with a good-natured someone who admits that, yes, she won the lottery. It's just a fact. I won the lottery. Toni Morrison was admitting that, indeed, yes, she *was* Toni Morrison and was lucky and talented and a hard worker, and indeed a great writer, just as, in *Letters to a Young Poet,* Rilke eventually gets around to admitting that he is, indeed, Rilke. This feeling of artistic power—aesthetic triumphalism—seems to me to be increasingly rare in our time, but Toni Morrison has it, and it shows in her work.

May you be so talented. May you be so lucky. The result of *my* early failures is that I find writing to be almost unimaginably difficult. I always suspect that I am about to make a terrible set of mistakes. Therefore, the writing comes slowly, when it comes at all. I'm not by any stretch of the imagination, my imagination, prolific. It's good to be confident, but a lack of self-confidence can be turned to your own purposes if it helps you to take pains, to take care, to avoid glibness.

Thomas Mann said, "A writer is someone for whom writing is more difficult than it is for other people."

About four years ago I started to receive anonymous postcards signed "The New Philistine." Almost every time a new story of mine would appear somewhere in print, I'd get a postcard with a withering critical judgment about my efforts inscribed on it, signed by the anonymous Philistine, as he called himself. These cards were postmarked from Detroit. They were soon followed by copies of a 'zine, hand-published every few months, eponymously titled *The New Philistine.* Each issue contained attacks on my work and the work of my contemporaries. The attacks were rabid, funny, intelligent, unfair, wildly accurate and wildly inaccurate (one of the *NP*'s theories was that Tama Janowitz had undergone a sex change of some sort—I was never clear about exactly what it was, or how), maniacal, vicious, crazed, full of spirit and lunacy and anger.

Stung and amused by the 'zines and the postcards, I discovered at the bottom of one of the issues a name and a phone number and an address. After all, the Philistine wanted subscribers. I called him. A man with a somewhat blank voice answered the phone.

"It's Charles Baxter," I said.

"Oh," he said. "It's you?"

"I'm calling because I have a question."

"What?"

"Why me?"

"Why not you?" he said.

"That's no answer."

"Okay. Why you? You *personally?* Well, because you write about Detroit without knowing anything about it, for one thing. I work there. My life would kill you. And you have all this power."

"That's ridiculous."

"No, it isn't."

We argued about that for a while. We hung up. But we ended up corresponding for a while, and I subscribed to his 'zine and gave him some money. He went on relentlessly attacking me and all my works, though other writers—Jay McInerney in particular—were abused more severely than I was. He wrote some wonderful nonfiction—one essay in particular about American ballparks—that appeared in other magazines, and which I nominated for *The Pushcart Prize Anthology.* He sent me part of his novel, which I read.

He was full of the Holy Spirit, crazed with writing and reading. He worked as a bartender on Cass Avenue, and his interior life resembled that of an eighteenth-century polemicist and pamphleteer at the end of his rope. After a while, he dropped out of sight. I haven't heard from him in years. I think about him all the time. I hope he's still writing.

You have all that power.

I do?

What if I say this: All right, I have it, but it's not mine. I don't have a *claim* on it. Native Americans thought that you couldn't own land, because land wasn't yours to own. Any talent, any gift, any art, can leave you. I've done my best to learn a craft, which is like acquiring a set of tools. And what power anyone can acquire, anyone can lose. Fiction writers don't necessarily get better as they get older. Frequently, they get worse.

You do what you can. You wait, in readiness. You try to be modest. You try not to destroy yourself with drugs and drink and sex and selfishness. You are grateful for what you get, knowing that it could be much, much worse.

It's still very quiet here, and it's still snowing, of course, and the waves are higher, and it's the next day, and as you know perfectly well, I lied to you: I have a second pair of glasses, and I have been watching these words, each letter and phrase, as they appeared on the screen, and I've been changing them and correcting them minute by minute, hour by hour, day by day, because that is who I am, and that is what I do.

Blessings,
Charles Baxter

Ann Beattie

Ann Beattie's twelfth book, *Park City: New and Selected Stories,* was published by Knopf in June 1998. She lives with her husband in Maine and Key West and is at work on a new novel.

A primer for responding to all those nonwriters who would write if they had time, and a bountiful lesson on why you are so different from them.

Letter to a Young Fiction Writer

If I had not been asked to offer some thoughts to someone starting their career, I feel sure I would not be writing the words I am about to write. And the reason is really inextricable from one of the most important things I can say: you must do your own work—the work you are compelled to do—rather than capitulating, and letting your arms be twisted like Gumby's. There is only so much time, and you have only so much energy (and, I hope, a little more than you think, because you'll need that to carry you through), and your obligation is to yourself, and to your work. I suppose it is also to your family, and even to the family dog, but it has to stop within some—what to call it?—intimate distance from yourself. It took me a long while to catch on to the fact that I was expected to justify myself, and in so doing, to (impossible task) quell the questioner's anxiety. What I mean is that curious people—perfectly okay to be curious; also perfectly okay to pass on other peoples' curiosity—will want to know if you write every day, what your writing habits are, whether you take characters from so-called real life, etc. They are asking because they want to hear that on some level—and they will clutch at the most tenuous filament—what you do is just a version of what they do. It isn't. I'm not saying it's better or worse, I'm just saying that it's a false premise that leads them, and you, into a limbo that you don't want to be in. There's enough confusion in writing, let alone in trying to make that confusion comprehensible to someone who's never even tried it—though the entire world means to write one day, you know. They already have pithy diary entries, they are still proud of a paper they wrote on Robert Frost's poetry in Freshman English that they got an A on, and a few of them have recently written letters that were published in the local newspaper. And by the way: what are *you* doing for the manatees? People want to think that what you do is not magical. That it is not far removed from the kind of thinking, and imagining, they themselves experience. I wouldn't know about the latter (though I do observe that whatever they are feeling, they think about writing, but usually do not write), but about the former, I am sure: it is magical. If you tell them this bluntly, at best they will think you're loony, and at worst they'll think you're having them on—just another one of those fanciful, teasing, unrespectful writers. You know, their worst fear of writers. When they say, "I'm going to tell you about what happened to me Saturday, but you can't write this," what they're really saying is not that they fear their story will be stolen, but that there is no mediational magic, no transformation involved in what *you* do. They may also be afraid that their story—their life, by extension—isn't worth stealing. It is not your responsibility to make them feel better by writing it, of course, but it is also not your responsibility to listen to their story, since you are not a story repository. Guard your freedom and your space. You will need it.

I see that I have jumped in and mentioned problematic things, or things to which I feel I have had to become inured. Other people may not be push-overs the way I am (how can you write without being vulnerable?). Other people may simply have happier experiences from conversations with non-writers. I did, too, when I started out, and perhaps what has happened is that as I've gained a reputation (I leave myself wide open for the appropriate snorts here), people's anxiety, or simply their desire, has also increased exponentially. I am doing what they want to do. I am—or Mavis Gallant is, or Alice Munro is—who they want to be. And they think or hope that by figuring me out—they hope with my putting them at ease, concerning inspiration and writing methods, and other much less tangible things, as I mentioned before—they will be able to move into my position. I don't think that this is often assumed with malice. People who have any sense, however faulty, of what it is to be a writer in the United States usually are sophisticated enough to know that you don't topple the person who's king of the hill and then stand there, occupying his or her position. They understand that their days in the schoolyard are gone, yet they think that there is a society of writers where there are brilliant thoughts and exciting parties with drinks and delicacies, and that if they were part of this secret society, they would be annointed. They are correct about the drinks. About the rest, they are deluded. I can think of very few places that writers congregate, and if they do, they will not be in that place talking about their writing, but about things people always talk about everywhere. There's nothing to join. I have to admit that in retrospect, I guess I did think there were things to join—at least more than I'm a joiner now. I was never used to being part of organizations, but in college I was part of the arty crowd, and when I opted out of the workaday world and its securities and miseries, I was part of the hippie world. For a while, I thought I was part of the *"New Yorker"* world, and to a small extent, I was: I became a writer with a first reading agreement. (This was during the editorship of the estimable William Shawn; they got to see everything first, in exchange for higher payment if they took a story.) I was a literary twosome with Roger Angell, whose wonderful editing and encouragement I will always be grateful for; I was admitted to, and came to be recognized at, book publication parties, of which I have attended approximately six in my lifetime, and that was that. I didn't live in New York. I lived in a small town in Connecticut that I once put into a short story by name, and received a query in the margin of the story when the *New Yorker* sent me the galleys, saying: "No such place." But yeah; there was such a place. It was a crossroads, and there was a used car lot across the street from the room in which I wrote, and every day, as I looked at the cars, I thought, *I am going to write my way out of here.*

I did. In a sense, I'm still writing my way out, though now I'm writing myself out of the palm trees that tickle my computer screen (I'm not kidding) in Key West, where I can easily pretend it isn't winter. I've got pals here, which I've always been lucky to have—so many people took an interest in my work early on and encouraged me that I almost can't believe my good luck. I remember their good feedback very, very well—and I don't feel as isolated as I once felt, but now I can't as easily impose on people (oh, I do; my loyal first readers are still there, but I mean on a daily basis) because I've found out what that imposition means. What sort of toll it takes. My mailbox is a landslide of galleys that writers and editors want blurbs for; I sit on literary committees that require a large amount of time to do the reading and thinking and conferring. I could go on, but what I do is neither harder nor easier than what any working person does. Still, it's made me cautious about intruding on other writers' time.

The best things about making it as a free-lance writer? The thrill of beating the odds, though when I started, I had no idea what I was up against, so that made it easier. When I published, I had no personal relationship with any other writer. The miraculous fact that up to this point, I've made enough money to support myself. I mention those two things first, because they're important, but I want to get them out of the way. More important is the freedom. I have no particular talent for gardening, but if I could avoid being a 9–5er and tend my garden, I'd feel pretty exhilarated about that, I'm sure. But getting to write . . . first and foremost, I have the time and the security—the security in part simple good luck, but a good part, also, arranged for by me: no children (love that Goddaughter); no pets (a borrowed dog every summer); few plants (UPS'd back and forth between houses); painter husband who's a workaholic, but an *understanding,* tolerant, bemused workaholic . . . well: I've got the time, and the context, to do what matters deeply to me.

But by way of advice? What can I say—don't make mistakes? Hardly likely. There's also the argument that they do you good, but that seems to me a little like the pro red wine argument. You know: good if taken in moderation; does more for men than women, healthwise.

Find the time to write. Protect the time to write. Be inventive: get gorgons. Forget e-mail. Whatever it takes. Because you'll still need more time than there is, and also it's important to leave enough time to waste. That's one of the many reasons the stereotype of the writer with the bottle holds, though the creative wasting of time is not only more fun, but nobler. Don't let people persuade you to talk away your material, and don't let them persuade themselves that you are only another version of them (I suppose it's a harmless delusion for them, but don't be around when they're stating the ostensible similarities. Such comparisons kill brain cells). Hope for luck, wish to turn out to be photogenic, pray that the mess that book publishing is in may eventually result in something good (we already have the appearance of the excellent Dalkey Archive Press, which publishes and re-publishes important, serious literature). May the road rise with you. . . . Just kidding. Put out of your mind my advice and anyone else's and listen to that inner voice. It will even prevail over the inner child, that will tell you to go running and screaming away from writing, directly to the playground.

People who do not write will tell you that they haven't gotten around to it yet because they know they can do it. They just need to get the kids in school, hire a lawn service and spend weekends writing, re-cycle their notebooks into useable material, make a concerted effort to remember their dreams. It can be done tomorrow. Any time. They are just about to get to it—that thing that comes so naturally to all of us, that thing we've all done all through school and with great elan in our love letters. The books they could write, their plots based on something that happened to them, that are more exciting than le Carré's. Tomorrow. Tomorrow. I'll see you tomorrow.

They are not writing because they can. You are writing because you can't.

—Ann Beattie

Ray Bradbury

Since his *Martian Chronicles* of almost fifty years ago, Mr. Bradbury's work has been synonymous with lyricism, an abiding focus on human (as well as interstellar) relationships, and—as with his *Fahrenheit 451*—the survival of language and liberty.

Bradbury addresses, here, a high-school boy (who would become a novelist and professor), and he gives the advice of one who is, above all else, a writer.

Dear Dan Chaon

April 30/May 1, 1982

Dear Dan Chaon:

This, written on the train crossing New Mexico on my way home from 3 weeks travel, to Washington, D.C., Bowling Green, Ohio, New York, etc. Lecturing, and tending to business. I carried your BICKERSTAFF story along, hoping to have time to read it, and comment. So now's the time . . .

I enjoyed it, immensely. Your style, as ever, is on the nose . . . evocative, imaginative, clever.

The story is a small gem, and perhaps, as with your other stories, too small. I can see it in some quarterly review, but you DO want to move out into that larger world of the fantasy and s.f. magazines, don't you? Study the current issues. Read all of the back ones you can find, and, of course, read all the anthologies in your library, if they have a decent supply. You must find a way to write longer stories, with a broader framework. Who, for instance, is MR. BICKERSTAFF? where did he come from, where was he going, what was his life? Why is this happening to him. It seems to me your story should start earlier, before he arrives at the bus-stop, with premonitions of Doom, along the way. Has he done some thing to deserve his Fate, or, like most of us, at times, is he simply run down, like someone in the street? There are thousands of undeserved deaths every day in all countries . . . a man killed by cancer here, a man gored by a bull there, a woman decapitated when an iron beam thrusts through her car window—sheerest coincidence. I guess I'm asking you the point of your story? Are you sure you have clarified it for *us*? for *you*? Is it a comment, via metaphor, on life? Shouldn't you fill in on Mr. B's previous life a bit? You are working here a bit in the vein of Franz Kafka, whose work shouldn't be imitated, it's far too forceful and strange and, let's face it, if he were sending out his stories today, he would have as much trouble selling them as when he lived.

Anyway, take a look at your structure here. What magazine did the story appear in? If it was a small college mag., you could still, as a rewritten tale, send it to MAGAZINE OF FANTASY & S.F.

What does Mr. B want from life? I guess you have left that out. My characters write my stories for me. They tell me what they want, then I tell them to go get it, and I follow as they run, working at my typing as they rush to their destiny. Montag, in F.451 wanted to stop burning books. Go stop it! I said. He ran to do just that. I followed, typing. Ahab, in MOBY DICK, wanted to chase and kill a whale. He rushed raving off to do so. Melville followed, writing the novel with a harpoon on the flesh of the damned Whale!

Thanks for the poems, too. Very nice. But poetry is hard to comment on, criticise. I would prefer to be helpful with fiction.

Why are you going to college? If you aren't careful, it will cut across your writing time, stop your writing stories. Is *that* what you want? *Think. Do* you want to be a writer for a lifetime? What will you take in college that will help you be a writer? You already have a full style. All you need now is practise at structure. Write back. *Soon.* Luck to you!

R. Bradbury.

David Bradley

David Bradley received a B.A. in Creative Writing from the University
of Pennsylvania (1972) and an M.A. in United States Studies from
the University of London (1974). He is the author of two novels:
South Street (1975) and *The Chaneysville Incident* (1981), which was
awarded the 1982 PEN/Faulkner Prize and an Academy Award from
the American Academy and Institute of Arts and Letters. His nonfiction has appeared in such publications as *Esquire, Redbook,* the *New
York Times,* the *Los Angeles Times,* and the *New Yorker.* He has been
a recipient of fellowships from the John Simon Guggenheim
Foundation and the National Endowment for the Arts, and is currently completing a nonfiction book, *The Bondage Hypothesis:
Meditations on Race, History and America.*

*A generous meditation on the difficulties
of being—of thinking of oneself as—an artist.*

Letter to a Writer

Dear Kel—

Once again we've managed to meet and part without discussing We-Both-Know-What. We've gotten very good at this. We sit down to have a drink and a talk. The dread subject comes up. Neither of us *brings* it up; it just sort of . . . arises. Our voices rise, too, and our diction gets clipped. But, hearing the timbre of our voices, we both realize we are about to hit some kind of wall—not merely hit it, but run into it at full tilt. So we sheer off. We change the subject.

In terms of being polite, this is a good idea, because at this point we are both likely to say something we will regret—something else, in my case; I've already said one thing I'd love to take back. In terms of being friends, it's not a good idea. Because what we are not talking about is something which has brought us both pleasure and joy, and which is so important to me—and I believe, to you—that we cannot truly *be* friends unless we share it in some way. At least we have to talk about it.

God, you'd think it was sex.

Maybe it should be sex, given the libidinous reputation of the writers' workshop where we met. Somebody told me a story in the *New York Times* called the place "Bedloaf"; if so, the *Times* missed the point—as it so often does. Sure, some folks were playing musical cots and more were thinking about it, and almost everybody was involved in episodes of drunken debauchery, but during all of it—well during almost all of it—what they were doing with Priapismic urgency was talking about what they did and how they did it. The night we met folks were in a frolicky frame of mind—some of those dances were pretty creative. And admittedly we only found

ourselves together on the porch because the DJ started playing things that were, in our opinion, undancetoable. But while
we were there we did discuss a few matters of literary signif-
icance—and it wasn't easy in the face of megawatts of amplification. And later, during other conversations, we actually
exchanged some significant information about how we felt
about writing. We knew little about each other as writers, but
we were able to talk about writing, then. Now, we almost hit
a wall. The reason for that is, I think, that at the writers' workshop we were both writers.

Obviously, we were not equals. You were a "Contributor,"
which is to say you were among the group who had asked to
be there and who were paying for the privilege. I was a member of the "Faculty," which is to say I was among the group
who had been asked to be there who were getting paid. I
admit, this seems a serious disparity, especially as the workshop we were attending has all those not-so-subtle gradations
between Contributor and Faculty. But there's an advantage to
the system: it gives writers of different levels of experience
the chance to be near the top of *some* pecking order.

It made you and me, for example, more, rather than less,
equal. For among the Contributors you were a rising star.
You'd had some pieces published, even gotten paid for them
a time or two. I, among the Faculty, was merely one star in a
glittering constellation—and no supernova, either.

I'm not being modest—you know me better than that. But
it was a distinguished Faculty, and while I am not lacking in
distinction, I was—and am—lacking in *recent* distinction.
Proof: when we met, you knew all about my Faculty colleague
who had recently won the National Book Award, you'd read
her work, and sought her out for conversation. Of me, you'd
never even heard, had never read a word I'd written, and had

you not sought refuge from what some deluded DJ called dance music, we might never have conversed at all.

So what mattered, when we began to talk, was not our relative status but the fact that we both had earned our places at the workshop by writing. So had everybody else. Though there was a lot of pecking—also a few outright pissing contests—nobody questioned whether or not anybody was a writer. If you weren't, you wouldn't have been there. If you weren't, you wouldn't have *wanted* to be there. Everybody was legitimate. And while some might argue the Contributors actually purchased that legitimacy, I would rebut that in the literary world, the line between who pays and who gets paid is pretty fuzzy. I've "contributed" to quarterlies that paid little or nothing, and shortly after receiving the letter of acceptance—and before publication—received also a letter "inviting" me to subscribe.

Unfortunately, many would agree with what some would argue. American society doesn't like writers, but loves to pass judgment on a writer's legitimacy, and, worse, it uses piss-poor criteria, like how frequently and/or lucratively your work is published. Actually, it's a broader problem. Here we have a society which supposedly reveres those who have not merely ambitions, but dreams. At the same time, society has a pejorative term for persons of mature years who do dream of becoming something other than they are. The term is "wannabe."

It's okay to be a wannabe when you're seven years old. (*Whadayawannabe* when you grow up? adults ask kids. Previously Acceptable Answers: Iwannabe president, Iwannabe whatever Daddy was and Iwannabe like Mickey Mantle. Currently Acceptable Answer: I wannabe like Mike.) By the time you're a teen-ager, though, you can't just wannabe; you're supposed to be On Your Way. By the time you're twenty-five, thirty at the latest, you're supposed to be highballing on the Career Track—preferably the "fast track." You don't have to be the boss, but you better be giving orders to *somebody*.

This timetable is appropriate to many endeavors, necessary to some. (Mike got to be Mike because he started working his butt off as soon as he got cut by his high school coach; he'd never have made it if he'd waited until he was in college, because he might never have made it to college. And he'd look stupid if, at thirty-five, he was out there in short pants still trying to make the team.) But it is totally inappropriate to writing, because developing as a writer takes a long time. Oh, if you got rejected by your high school literary magazine and started working as hard as Mike did to develop your skills, you could write a publishable novel by the time you're twenty-five. Only you probably hadn't read enough literature in a disciplined and systematic enough fashion to know what skills to develop. Most people don't get taught to read critically until they're in college—if then.

The gross result is, by the time most writers figure out they want to be writers, they are beyond the age when we expect people to be at the elementary levels of anything. And rather than respecting their dreams, society makes quiet fun of them. Even sportswriters made quiet fun of Mike, when he decided he wanted to be like Mickey; guys who warmed the bench in Little League were criticizing the man because he was only—only!—playing triple-A ball.

And Mike was lucky; he may have been a minor-leaguer, but he was still a pro. The wannabe writer not only doesn't get paid (usually), he or she has to pay for coaching. Most promising athletes get coaching for free. Most professions pay bright prospects to develop their skills in "entry-level positions." There are no such positions in writing. Which means wannabe writers have no *professional* identity, which, in America, means they have no legitimacy. If you say you're an amateur golfer, that means you are a golfer who has to pay to play. (Like even Mike does.) You say you're an amateur writer, that means you aren't a writer; you're just a wannabe.

If you say you are a professional writer you get the social equivalent of an FBI background check. You know I used to be a college professor. One of the things I liked about that was, I could tell people what I did and nobody asked me to prove it. Since I've started putting "writer" in the little box that says "occupation," everybody from the Internal Revenue Service to the trophy wife at the cocktail party to the guy next to me on the plane wants to examine my credentials.

There I'll be, tray table in its full downright and unlocked position, tapping away on my Macintosh™ when the guy in the next seat finishes going over his presentation or marking up his contract or proving what a jerk he is by making a phone call—I mean, you know how much that costs? Anyway, he'll watch me for a minute and then say, So, you some kind of writer? Now that's not obnoxious; he's actually being polite. What he wants to know is, should he leave me alone because I'm engaged in a revenue-producing exercise (A/K/A work) or can he interrupt me because I'm playing some weird version of computer solitaire. (You'd be surprised how many high-powered executives use their high-end laptops to play games at angels thirty-five.) Anyway, I'll say, Yeah, I'm some kind of writer. So he'll say, Who do I write *for*? I'll say I'm freelance. Which he'll interpret as "wannabe," because if I was *really* a writer I'd have a *job*. And a boss. Especially a boss. (I mean, how can you be legitimate if you don't have a designated ass to kiss?) So next comes the question, with a real suspicious tone: "Really." Pause. "Have you *published* anything?"

When that happens, I feel like saying, "You're a doctor? Really? You treated any patients? You're a lawyer? You try a case?" I don't say anything so obnoxious . . . usually. But there was this slick stockbroker-type who asked the question when I just happened to have a piece in that month's *Esquire,* which they just happened to have on the plane . . . That boy bought me drinks all the way to Dallas–Fort Worth. And there was this . . . *woman* at a cocktail party. Somebody's third wife, not-yet-thirty-anything, blonde-over-blue, two-hundred-dollar hair-do, body by personal trainer, a junior college drop-out who'd been the firm's receptionist before she became the latest Mrs. M & A Attorney. She was raving about the latest Danielle Steele (in hardcover, of course) when somebody said I was a writer. She looks me up and down and says, "Have you written anything I could have read?" She really had to work to get that grammar right. So I look her up and down and say, "Well, you may have tried . . ."

Well. The point is, when the question gets asked, some of us writers can answer Yes, but some of us must answer No, and then there's nothing you *can* say, because you're in that wannabe category, along with that poor jerk Billy Joel sings about, Paul, the real estate/novelist. And some of us mumble apologetically because while they have been published it wasn't in any place impressive to anybody. What they ought to do is look the jerk in the eye and say, "So, you're a pilot in the Strategic Air Command? You ever drop one of those H-bombs, or are you still just flying training missions?"

That's you. And I think that's maybe the mortar of the wall we almost run into. At the writers' workshop, we could both say we were writers; in fact, it went without saying. Out here, I can say it, and, if necessary, defend the claim. You can't. Out here, I'm Chevy Chase . . . and you're not.

I hope you're not too young to get that joke. And I hope you understand that I understand: for you, this is no joking matter. Nor is it for any writer, because all of us from time to time have to fight to sustain our writerly identities. I'm not talking about ego. I'm talking about the sense that you *are* a writer, or that, if you're still in the wannabe stage, that you are *becoming* a writer, not just futzing around. If you have that sense, it doesn't matter what anybody thinks. It doesn't matter if the IRS doesn't think you need a home office, or if the guy in 5A thinks you're full of crap, or if the trophy wife who never heard of you wrote her Ph.D. dissertation on something you only wish you could have written by a writer you would kill to be even a little like.

It doesn't even matter what *you* think. Which is important, because we all have periods when we think we're getting nowhere, never have gotten anywhere, never will get anywhere, and who the hell are we to cast aspersions on Danielle Steele? At least she cranks 'em out. Nobody asks her if she's published. So what if she's not William Fucking Shakespeare? We're not William Fucking Shakespeare, either. Are we kidding ourselves here? Should we maybe get a real job? All writers ask themselves such questions, but for some of us they are purely rhetorical. For others of us, they are not. I think that's maybe part of the wall. If so, the wall has gotten higher since we first saw it looming.

You know the outline of my transition. I hope you don't need the details; I'd hate to think I wasted any of our time together whining. The story line is, when I was young I started teaching at a university. Over the next twenty years I went from teaching freshman comp part-time to teaching graduate-level creative writing full-time. Then I got fired.

Why I got fired is . . . embarrassing. I mean, I didn't do anything scandalous, or even interesting; I wish I had, at least I could get a story out of it. As it is, all I got was a right-to-sue letter from the Equal Opportunity Employment Commission, and, trust me, that is not a dramatic plot development. Nor was there a lot of emotional drama. Usually when some poor Joe gets canned from a job he's had for twenty years, he gets a little depressed, because he's come to identify himself with the job or the company. I didn't.

Oh, I had a bad few days at the beginning of September when, for the first time in twenty years, I wasn't walking into a classroom. And I still miss what happens in creative writing classrooms. (Why not? Basically, I was getting paid to talk shop, and work with texts, and in the process I was learning a lot about the craft that I might have had to pay somebody to teach me otherwise.) At first I missed the rhythm of academia and I still miss the interplay of long-term instruction, but I never missed *me*. When I wandered into the groves of academe I was already a writer, in both the private and the public sense; I'd never have gotten hired if I hadn't already had a novel published. But after I was hired, I didn't become a professor. I was just a writer who'd lucked into a job with a high income-to-freedom ratio. I liked teaching. I worked hard at it. I became good at it. But I was never dedicated to it. I surely never wanted to be a professor. So when I wasn't Professor Bradley anymore, frankly, my dear, I didn't give a damn.

I give less now. Because I've discovered I feel more like a writer, and that makes it easier to write. I have more time to write, and writing is the way I get what I need. Well, most of

what I need. To the extent I need a public identity, I must create and maintain it by writing. I am close to broke most of the
time—actually, we freelance writers don't call it broke, we call
it a "temporary cash-flow difficulty"—but writers are *supposed* to be broke, and the solution to my financial problems
is to write my way out of them. In fact, I feel—maybe I'm
crazy—that the solution to *all* my problems is to write my
way, if not out of them, then through them. (Hey, I'm writing
to *you*, no?)

I'm not saying I feel lucky to have been fired. It was trau-
matic and embarrassing and expensive and infuriatingly
unjustified. But I do feel lucky that, when I get up in the
morning, what I'm supposed to do is what I wanted to do,
and that I don't even have to feel guilty about it.

You do.

You didn't when we met. Then you were, as the actors say,
between engagements. You'd given up your previous engagement to attend to the ultimate family business; you'd been
there when you were needed. Now, in practical terms, that
business was done. You had to deal with grief, but you'd
found that writing helped with that. And you didn't have to
feel guilty about doing what you wanted to do because you
had just done an admirably right and unselfish thing. So you
were writing. You were in a writers' group. Your writing was
being accepted. *You* were being accepted as a writer. You
were attending the writers' workshop. You had lots of cues
telling you that you were a writer. Now you have lots of cues
reminding you that you are not.

Now you have a new professional engagement. Now you
work in a laboratory, not a workshop, live in a city where you
lived and worked before you decided you wanted to be a
writer. Lots of people know you; few know you as any kind of

writer. They accept you as the person you were before: an experienced researcher, not an inexperienced writer. If your colleagues know about your writing, they think of it as a hobby—something properly consigned to evenings and week-ends, something you can and should put aside whenever professional considerations require. Your friends and family may honestly want you to do what you want to do, but they also want you to do what they want you to do. They want you to do things for them. Worse, they want you to do things *with* them—go to lunch, go for a drink, go to the movies. They may accept it if you say you won't have time for a while, but they'll want to know how long it's going to be. They will probably not accept the answer a writer *has* to give: It may be quite a while. In fact, it may be forever.

The cues you are getting are accurate. You are not much of a writer according to society's criteria. You *are* a biological researcher. You get paid to do all those technical things I can't even pronounce and you are good at them. The demands these people make are legitimate. You do have responsibilities to job, to friends, to family. You do have to take your cat to the vet. The time you spend doing what you want to do *is* time you could be spending with others. All of which means, it's hard for you to *feel* like a writer.

Oh, sure, you *think* of yourself as a writer. But that private identity, that sense of self and purpose, is hard to maintain in the face of the terms of your life. It's hard to maintain in the face of your writing; you know what you are doing when you are not writing; when you are, you are often frustrated and confused. And that makes it harder for you to do the one thing that makes you feel most like a writer: write. When I see that wall looming I wonder if part of it is that you feel guilty because it's been a while since you actually wrote anything.

If it has been a while, understand, I am not being critical. But how much we write (or don't write) is something all writers have to think about, and that wannabe writers have to think about especially hard. When I was a professor, I found it easy to get sucked into working long and hard at legitimate tasks that produced income . . . but weren't writing. I don't mean teaching, I mean dumb stuff, like being the chair of the hiring committee. Teaching was especially seductive, because when I was making notes on some student's manuscript it *felt* like I was writing. But I wasn't. Eventually, I figured that out. I never figured out what to do about it.

Maybe I am lucky to have been fired. Now I get up in the morning and go to work at my word-processor, and if I put in only half a normal American workday, I've been writing for four hours.

You get up and go to work at your High Pressure Liquid Chromatograph or your ELISA Plate Reader (whoever the hell Elisa is) and at the end of your day you have been not-writing for eight hours. So it's after work, now you've got time to write, and maybe even something specific you want to work on, but do you have the energy? Maybe you just aren't in the *mood*.

And there's nothing to force you into the mood. Nobody *cares* if you write or not. Your friends don't care; they knew you before you started writing seriously, and may even have felt more comfortable around you then. Your family doesn't care; they just want you—and themselves—to be happy. Your cat doesn't care. Your boss doesn't care. And on those days when the writing is difficult the questions you ask yourself are not rhetorical. Why *should* you bust your butt when you may be kidding yourself and, even if you aren't, the confirmation and meager rewards are at best years away? Why *should* you tap on a keyboard, wrestling sense out of balky sentences, when you can pet the cat and he purrs?

Whenever I see that wall looming, I wonder if part of it isn't the fact that, every day, I get to do what I want to do, and I get to do what *you* want to do. I'm not saying you are not dedicated to, or, at least, conscientious about, your research work; I know you are. I'm not saying I do not respect the value of that work; I do. But I don't want to be a biological researcher. I do not go off to biological research conferences. You do want to be a writer. You do go off to writers' workshops. And so I wonder, when we are talking and I make casual references to my life—to editors, to magazines, other writers whom I know—I wonder if you do not . . . resent me a little. I would, if I were you.

I know what you do resent: the thing I said that I'd love to take back. You resent it so much you won't forget I said it, so much that you've forgotten some of the context—or at least it seemed that way the last time I tried to apologize. For the record: You'd gotten a letter rejecting a story you'd been working on for over a year.

You were angry because . . . well, because the story had been rejected, but also because the editor had made vague reference to the main character's being "under-developed." But you'd decided the piece was finished; the main character was developed enough for you. And . . . and you were angry.

Now as you *may* remember—ahem—I agreed with you. After all (I did say this) it's your story. You have the right to decide when it's finished. It doesn't matter what some editor thinks unless the sonofabitch won't pay you if you don't make the changes he wants. Then it still doesn't matter unless you need the money. But since the magazine in question didn't pay anyway, screw him. If your only reward was going to be to have the piece published your way, it would be no reward at all to have it published any other way.

I should have stopped there.

But one thing I've learned during my years in this business is, you can sometimes extract useful information from the comments of even an unperceptive editor. Maybe this guy didn't know his elbow from a number two pencil, but at least he'd read the story; his comment had to indicate how some readers would respond.

Another thing I've learned is, while to say something is "under-developed" is a common editorial cop-out, to under-develop a piece is a common writerly failing. All pieces start out "under-developed." The earliest stages of revision mostly involve figuring out what ought to be there, but isn't, and putting it in. Learning to *look* at a piece and *see* what needs to be added is part of what wannabes have to learn in order to be. It follows that writers of lesser experience often end up sending stories out thinking that they are fully developed when they aren't.

I also know that one reason inexperienced writers get rejected is that they labor under a heavier burden of proof. The same editor might have had the same reaction to and made the same comment about a piece by an experienced writer but might also have accepted it, presuming that the necessary development would be done. Inexperienced writers don't get that presumption. Editors assume that what they see is all they are going to get, and reject the piece. It's not that they're stupid. It's that there is a difference between what a writer does and what an editor does. A story is like a baby—which is to say, an under-developed human being. Its parents may love it, but it is of no use to the world until it grows up. Editors may see what could be, but if it isn't there now, they throw out the baby with the bathwater.

I wasn't dumb enough to say any of this to you then. (And I know, you're thinking, Well, if you'd said *that* instead of what you did say, I wouldn't have . . . But it might have been worse. A writer who's just gotten a rejection slip is like a grizzly bear with infected hemorrhoids; any statement which might be construed as, Maybe the editor was right is unlikely to ease anybody's pain.) What I was dumb enough to do was ask a compound question about the main character: What was at stake for her? What did she want out of the situation? What was going to happen if she didn't get it? What was going to happen if she did?

I knew what I was doing. I was using an editorial technique that is based on the theory that, as a piece moves from the first to the final draft, it tends to go through predictable stages, in which it will exhibit certain characteristic flaws. The way a writer makes a work-in-progress actually progress is not to "correct" it, but to *think* about the flaws by asking certain critical questions. The questions don't change as you move from draft to draft, but the answers should. Eventually you should be able to say, simply and clearly, what the piece is about, why it has the form it has, why it starts where it starts, what's at stake for the characters, what compels them to behave as they do. If you can't answer the questions, you can't do productive revision because you don't know what to change to what. Once you can answer, you can revise quickly and productively.

This is a valuable technique for teachers because it keeps you from having to slog through pages of not-very-good prose just to offer a little insight, and maybe getting caught up in glaring but irrelevant errors. (Most teachers get hung up on correcting grammar, because grammar errors are so unambiguous. But grammar errors are often just by-products of other kinds of problems.) It also keeps a teacher from getting too involved in some student's story. Which should make students happy because they tend to be unreasonably paranoid about some teacher influencing their story. (It doesn't; often nothing does other than unqualified praise.)

But the technique has nothing to do with education. It's what *all* writers do, one way or another, when they are creating and revising their work. Inexperienced writers—and some writing teachers—are always going on about "finding a voice" or "developing a style," but learning to be a writer actually depends on finding and developing your own ways to interrogate yourself about the relationship between what you've written and what you intended to write. When experienced writers discuss their work-in-progress with each other (and most don't) what we want is for someone else to formulate the questions in a way that is new to us, so we can maybe come up with new answers. That's what we want from editors, and the best editors have developed their own techniques. (One brilliant editor used to make faint pencil checkmarks in the margin. He wouldn't tell you what they meant. Figuring that out was your job. He's retired now, alas.)

So that's what I was trying to do when I asked you the compound question. If the editor was right, I knew what you were going to say, because if a story element is critically under-developed, the writer doesn't know *what* to say. You didn't. Which is where the trouble started.

My fault. I should have known better than to put somebody like you in that position. You told me yourself, you were always an A-student. A-students aren't used to not knowing the answers. Writers are. Writers *like* not knowing the answers. Writers like figuring the answers out.

You do . . . when you're feeling like a writer. I remember an e-mail you sent after you had had a revelation about a story. Even in e-mailspeak I could tell you were excited and joyful. Also a little embarrassed. I got the impression the revelation came during . . . ahem, *post-coital* afterglow. If so, don't ever tell your lover—unless he's a writer. If he is, he will take it as a compliment that you did not leap out of bed and boot up the computer. I'm not saying figuring out something that's been bugging you for months is better than sex, but I've had sex that wasn't nearly as good. The point is, you know the thrill of suddenly seeing what you didn't see before.

But when we were having this conversation you weren't feeling like a writer. You were feeling like you *weren't* a writer. In a sense, you were trying not to be a writer, because you were interviewing for professional positions—which is to say, you were working hard at convincing others in your profession that you were a dedicated and experienced researcher, not a wannabe writer. And you'd just had an editor tell you you weren't a good enough writer to suit his taste. So now you had this . . . *writer-person* asking you a question, about some story you thought was finished, and though at some level you understood that not knowing the answer was no big deal, at another level you thought a real writer would know the answer. So you started feeling even less like a writer . . . and you really started getting mad.

I didn't see this—although I should have. So when you asked—a little angrily and very acidly—if it had not occurred to me that you might know the answer but merely be inarticulate, I said that for a writer to claim to be inarticulate was like a ballet dancer parking in a handicapped zone. Which made you even angrier, which is when you got all huffy about the fact that I hadn't actually *read* the piece.

I said, I didn't *need* to read it, and started explaining the technique, but when I got to the part about predictable stages and characteristic flaws you interrupted and asked if what I was saying was that you were just like every other writer. And I said the one thing I'd love to take back:

Yes.

Writing this out, I feel like I'm watching a train wreck in slow motion. I mean, how stupid could I be? Even if I couldn't remember how it was for me—and I can, I just forgot—I had enough experience as a teacher to know how writers—indeed, artists of all types—often get started: when some beloved authority figure—parent, teacher, favorite aunt, whomever—tells them they have a "gift," a "talent," something that sets them apart from all the other little kids, something that makes them *special*.

For most of us it is a singular moment that glows in our memories. I remember how it happened for me. (Although the glow was dimmed because I was young and overly religious, and when they said "talent" I thought they meant "talents" as in the parable in the Gospel According to St. Matthew, and if I didn't bust my little butt making my talent increase Jesus (Himself) Christ was going to order me cast into the outer darkness where there would be weeping and gnashing of teeth.) I know you. I remember how it happened for you, because you told me about it. And you told me the person who provided that critical confirmation was the one who meant the most to you then, and no doubt still does: your mother. You also told me that one of the last things you were able to tell her before she died was that you had been accepted by the writers' workshop—that was the last chance you had to make her proud. And she was proud. So here I am, six months later, saying, You're not special. You're just like everybody else.

Thank you for letting me live.

What I said was true. But—and I *know* this—in the very beginning, the "early wannabe" years, you cannot face that truth. Indeed, you have to refuse to face it. You have to insist on the myth of speciality, because in the beginning that's all you have. It's not just that nobody—yourself included—thinks you are a writer, it's that your writing really isn't much good. That's the truth you do have to face. In fact, the extent to which you recognize how bad you are is a better indication of whether you will ever be more than a wannabe than is the quality of your writing; at the beginning your literary taste has to be well ahead of your literary ability. All that can sustain you when you read the *drek* you've written is faith in your potential. If you don't have that, every time you pick up something by a writer you admire, you will be totally discouraged.

I am not guessing here. It was while reading *Absalom, Absalom!* for about the third time that I really understood what kind of writer I wanted to be. Then I found I couldn't write for a month, because I also understood that he was William Faulkner, and I wasn't. I should have remembered that and lied to you.

Why didn't I lie? I don't know, really. God knows, I lied about this when I was a teacher. Well, actually, I avoided the question. Maybe I was overly impressed by your success, and thought you were further along in the process of becoming a writer than you actually were—I thought you could take it, in other words. (Actually, I think you could have taken it if you hadn't been in circumstances that were weakening your sense of writerly identity.) Or maybe I was self-absorbed; at the time I was all excited about rediscovering my writerly identity. I was busy not-teaching, and you were not then and never had been my student. That's no excuse. I'm sorry. I should have lied . . . then.

Maybe I should lie now. But each time I see that wall looming I think of all the things you will need to understand and accept as you become less a wannabe and more a writer. I'm not just talking craft, I'm talking internal psychic changes, alterations in your point of view that, while necessary, can be painful and confusing and depressing as hell. It's hard to get through it without a guide who's been through it, or a cohort who is going through it with you. I had guides—good ones—but still there were times . . . Well. The point is, I worry that you don't. Each time we approach the wall I think that, if I am truly your friend, I should not sheer off. And since I've already given voice to one of the hardest things to accept, I might as well say it again: You are not special.

I am not saying you do not have talent. I think you do. Which is something I would *never* say to a student. Because I also know how dangerous relying on talent can be. If we never get beyond the wall, if you never hear anything else I say about writing, please hear this: the level of talent is only a minor factor in calculating the probability that a wannabe writer will become a writer. Talent may influence how good a writer you ultimately become, or how quickly you master certain technical aspects of the craft, but there are so many other factors that even a great deal of talent quickly becomes unimportant . . . thank God. Because wanting to be a writer is a dream. Dreams can't depend entirely on any *a priori* for their realization. The most dramatic and wonderful dreams are those that fly into the face of the greatest obstacles.

You—like (I'm sorry) almost every wannabe—started writing because somebody you revered said you had talent. In your case—as in (I'm sorry) most cases—it was said a long time ago, which makes it more intense; writing is a dream deferred, ripened in the sun. The question is, what happens when somebody else you revere says you don't have talent? Do you quit? If the answer is yes, quit now because sooner or later somebody probably will say it. If the answer is no, then quit worrying about how much talent you have and start worrying about how much writing you're doing. And even if nobody ever says it, thinking your talent is important can make you feel inadequate if the writing doesn't come easily—and it won't, at some point. Then you'll sit there, all depressed, and think, Here I am with all this God-given talent and what have I done? Better to think you have only minor talent and have to work yourself silly to make up for the deficiency. After ten years you will be declared talented, probably by the same folks who told you otherwise.

Even then, you won't be special. But by then you won't want to be. By then you will take comfort in knowing that countless other writers have tried to solve the same problems you are trying to solve. By then you will rejoice that you can learn from their successes and their failures. Some say writing is a lonely business, and it is—if you insist on being special. But if you give that up you will realize how many others have sat working just as you do. And you will realize writers haven't been *alone* since . . . Chaucer. (Wannabe writers haven't been alone since Shakespeare, who started out to be a Catholic priest.)

Consider that something of a sales pitch; a preview of what I can offer you if we ever get beyond that wall. I'm not talking advice—I'm talking about ways of looking at things that may help you develop what the mental health professionals call coping strategies. Another preview: a brief meditation on time.

You (and about a thousand other writers) have said that being in your late thirties, you often feel you're just too far *behind.* You are behind in experience. There's no way around that. A lot of what you need to learn must be learned by trial-and-error. You have to make the errors. You can try to make them in a hurry, by writing a lot, but that only slightly alleviates the problem. Even praise doesn't really help; it's small comfort to you to know that, were you fifteen years younger and writing as well as you do, you would be hailed as a prodigy.

But writing is not a business of prodigies—I know, I was one. My first novel was published when I was twenty-five. The problem was, in order to write it I had used up all the life wisdom that I had. If I had written another novel in, say, two years, as I was expected to do, everybody would have been disappointed in it. *I* would have been disappointed.

What saved me was a phenomenon people in publishing were calling "The Sophomore Slump." Some bright young thing gets his or her first novel published to rave reviews, but the second one is lousy. (Actually the first one wasn't all that good, but first novels are, and should be, judged by different standards.) Anyway, I heard editors talking about the phenomenon and I decided, no sophomore slump for me. So I kept working on my second novel until I figured it was perfect, by which time I had—I didn't plan this—acquired the emotional understanding to make it look like a third novel. Of course that took years. By the time it was published, I wasn't a prodigy anymore.

Although it may not feel this way, it is an advantage that, while you are a young writer, you are not a young person. And you are not as far behind as you might feel, because much of what a writer needs to do are things you happen to have done.

You have, for example, read lots of books. Maybe you didn't read them as a writer learns to read them—writers have a hard time actually enjoying a book; we're too busy trying to figure out how it's working—but you have absorbed a lot of models, a lot of examples of what works and what doesn't. You may not have the theory, but you've amassed the data.

You have lived in lots of different places, which obviously gives you a choice of settings. You've met a lot of oddballs, hung out in a few bars. (One critic said my first novel sounded like I'd written it sitting on a barstool. She was trying to be nasty. I took it as a compliment. Besides, it was pretty much the truth.) You know how to do unusual things; you can ride a horse, run a pet shop, dissect various marine animals. You (like Mike) have competed in intercollegiate athletics. You've come in at four AM to make the donuts; you know what it feels like to be a five-foot-two-inch woman all alone in an empty shopping mall.

You've developed an area of expertise that has nothing to do with the craft of writing. This not only means you don't have to starve in a garret, but also gives you a set of conceptual analogies and problem-solving paradigms that you can draw on to develop your own understanding of the writing process. You've worked in an artistic form other than writing, and though you decided you didn't wannabe a photographer, you learned lessons about composition and balance, and . . . well, I don't know what you learned. My alternative field was music. But I do know how often I draw on what I learned while playing instruments and singing to get what I want out of a piece of writing.

More important, you have *lived.* You've been married and divorced and remarried. You've watched a beloved parent die. You've put a beloved pet to sleep. If you find your writing emotionally unsatisfying, it's not because it's so simplistic, but because you understand how complex emotions can be.

If it seems there isn't enough time, that's because there isn't. There isn't enough time for any writer. So writers have to learn to write when it looks like we aren't writing—when we're walking to work or riding the bus or flying in an airplane or driving to the grocery store. If you wait until you actually sit down at the machine before you start writing you are going to sit there staring at a blank something—a page, a screen—until you get yourself thoroughly depressed. That feeling of eagerness, the feeling that will have you rushing home from the lab to get something written down starts with the *idea*. Nobody fights for the time to get something written down if they don't have a clear idea of what that something is.

But if you are thinking always about the piece you are writing, or, better yet, a specific problem in that piece, if the questioning is always going on somewhere in your head, at amazingly regular intervals you will find yourself suddenly knowing what to do, and the idea itself will generate the will to do it. And even if you can't do it right that moment (those *post-coital* ideas are the best, but don't rush immediately to the keyboard), you will, at that moment, feel not like a wannabe but like a writer.

Understanding how critical that feeling is to your development is something else that lies beyond the wall. Because the fact is, you are going to be a wannabe for what will seem a long, long time. In fact, all writers are wannabes. We wannabe the author of whatever it is we are working on at the moment. And, since we assume—we *have* to assume—that whatever it is we are working on at the moment is gonnabe better than whatever we finished before, we all wannabe better writers. What you are, then, is a writer who—like every other writer—

is trying to become a better one. But in order to do that you have to have moments and situations in which you feel like a writer. And if they don't occur naturally, you have to invent them. You have to surround yourself with trappings and props to make yourself feel like you are a writer.

It's important, for example, that you have a singular physical place where *only* writing is done. I know, that's hard to handle in a one-room apartment, but it doesn't have to be an entire room. It can be a table in a corner on which you keep your writing implements—and which you use for nothing else. Not paying the bills. Not writing to friends. A space in which you don't read books, unless they are for research on a piece—in which you most emphatically do not read books about writing. What you have to create is a space in which you are the only writer whose writing matters.

And though it may seem self-serving for me to say this, you have to keep close to you people who see you as a writer. In this sense, new friends may be the best friends.

Since you have already had some success, it is vital that you continue to try to get your work published in the best places that will accept it. I know, I know, you now think that to have your work accepted by a so-called "amateur" magazine—what do you call them, 'zines?—is unimpressive. But getting published in some barely readable rag is the way almost all writers begin their public careers and it offers a chance to learn to deal with acceptance and publication rather than rejection. (Writers, by and large, have far too much practice at handling rejection, which is why pipsqueak editors can get away with kicking even the most august of us around.) And, I know, the most you ever got paid was twenty-five bucks. But, the first check almost all writers receive is of that order of magnitude. And I've never understood why it's more impressive to receive no payment for a piece published in a quarterly that is distributed to a few thousand subscribers, than to receive a small payment for a piece published in a shopper that is given way to twenty thousand consumers. So what if they get it for free? A lot of those who read quarterlies do it in libraries.

I'm not saying that to publish in 'zines and shoppers should be the zenith of literary ambition. I'm saying it is not the nadir of literary achievement, and that you have to give yourself the credit you deserve, because it is important that you remind yourself you are a writer because for a long time nobody else will.

But, most important, you have to write every day. Maybe you don't get to sit down at the keyboard for more than half an hour. Maybe you don't get to sit down at the keyboard at all. But you have to think about something you're writing or want to write. You have to make notes, or do some research. You have to do some writing task every day, because these acts are mutually reinforcing. The world does not yet know you as writer. Until it does, to write is the only reinforcement you can get, the only aspect of your career that you control. If you don't write on Tuesday you feel like less of a writer on Wednesday, and that makes it harder to justify writing on Wednesday. You can't go at your writing as single-mindedly as I now can. But you have to go at it as single-mindedly as *you* can. And if you feel you aren't doing enough writing, you aren't.

When I sat down to write this letter, I'd thought that now I'd write a paragraph telling you that, though you are not special as a wannabe writer, I felt you could become special, not because of your talent, but because you are a special person. I do not mean that in some smarmy, everybody's-special sense. Everybody *isn't* special. Even most wannabe writers are as uniform as an army of worms. But in your years of life you have developed a distinctive way of looking at the world. More, you have developed the habit of meditation; you think long and hard about what you see. That is far more important than having talent. I was going to say that, so I will, because it is true. But in the course of writing this something occurred to me: maybe the wall has nothing to do with your wanting to be a writer. Maybe you've discovered you don't want to be a writer after all.

It happens. I wish it happened more often. I would never tell anybody to stop dreaming, but there's nothing wrong with taking a good hard look at the realities and saying, I'm not going to make it in this incarnation. But when it does happen, it's hard. It's tough to be a wannabe, but it's harder to be a usetawannabe, at least for a few months.

It's hard because while society may make fun of wannabes, it vilifies quitters. It's hard because, if someone you love has told you you have a special talent, for you now to forsake it may seem like a repudiation of that person. It's hard because you have asked others to make allowances and even sacrifices for your ambition; now you're telling them not only your sacrifices, but theirs, have been wasted. It's hard because being a wannabe is exciting; there's a chance, at least, that there is more to your life than you once thought, that the future holds great possibilities. It's like you've got a lottery ticket for a big jackpot. It's one thing not to win, quite another to tear up the ticket before the drawing.

You can get over it. I've seen it done. It's not that, if you stop being a wannabe, you're nothing. (Most wannabes already are something. They just go back to being that alone.) Your family will be a lot happier with you. So will your old friends. So will your boss. The only people who might not be happier with you are your new friends—people who know you only or mostly as a wannabe writer, who may have been attracted to you because that's what you were. People who are themselves wannabe writers, or writers, and who either way are not about to give it up. All these friends you've made at writers' conferences. All these friends like . . . me.

When it came to me that this might be what the wall really is, I toyed with the idea of ending this letter with a little exercise in fictional license. I'd write that each time we've approached the wall, I've wanted to reach out and take your hand and say, But you know, this isn't *about* the writer that you are trying to become. This is about the person that you already are. The things about you that I value have nothing to do with my writing. I decided not to write that. Actually I decided not to write it three times.

The first time I decided not to write it because I was afraid you would hear it as a condescension. I wouldn't have meant it that way. I would have meant to take some of the *pressure* off; to allay any suspicion you might feel that I expect you to develop as a writer in a certain way, or in a certain time, and that, should you fail to follow that pattern, or even decide you do not want to develop as a writer at all, you would decline in my estimation and regard. (You wouldn't. Some of my best friends are not writers. Some of my best friends are writers—but I sometimes wonder why.)

I decided not to write it the second time because it *was* a condescension. Worse, an insult. I mean, if you were to say the things you value about me—I assume you do value some things about me—have nothing to do with my writing, I would feel you didn't understand what the hell I am all *about*. And I would reject your friendship, because I have dedicated too much of my life and my self to wanting to be a writer, becoming a writer, being a writer, to accept the regard of any-one who doesn't accept me as a writer first and foremost. Long before I earned a dime by writing, long before anything I wrote was published, long before I wrote anything publish-able, long before I wrote anything worthy of serious consid-eration, or even thoughtful rejection, I felt *I* deserved serious consideration. And I was angry when I didn't get it.

So should you be.

The third time I decided not to write it, I realized it would be a lie.

A lie because I do respect you as a person. And—libidinous reputation aside—we met at a writers' workshop, not at Club Med. By being there instead of at Club Med we were both making significant statements about ourselves, our lives, our ambitions. You were saying you wanted to be a writer. How can I claim to respect you as a person if I do not take you at your word? And if I, with whatever benevolent intent, were to take the pressure off, I would betray you by becoming part of a world that does not take you and your desire—and yes, your Goddamn *talent*—seriously.

So I'll end it this way: it matters to me whether or not you progress as a writer. Not because I want you to be a writer, but because that is what you want to be. Should that cease to be your dream, fine. But say so. Because until you say you don't wannabe any more, I will expect you to work at what you will write with the same diligence and dedication as I did when I was a wannabe, and as I still do. And we will talk about it. The next time we approach that wall, my friend, I will not sheer off. I hope you will not either. And I hope we both have airbags.

David

Rosellen Brown

Ms. Brown is the author of four novels, including *Before and After* and *Civil Wars;* three collections of poetry (most recently *Cora Fry's Pillow Book*); a book of short stories, *Street Games;* and a miscellany containing essays, poetry, and stories, *A Rosellen Brown Reader.* She teaches in the M.F.A. Program at the School of the Art Institute of Chicago.

Suggestions for learning to pay attention to the world, which is more our subject than we, ourselves.

You Are Not Here Long

Last year my friend the writer Carol Anshaw sent me *Four points for living a good life* which had been passed on to her by yet another friend (or maybe it was a therapist with a yen for elegant simplification), a sort of emotional chain letter. Looking at them through the lens of my own life as a writer I thought, Hmm, necessary if not exactly sufficient, these could form a fairly sound basis for a young (or should I say new?) writer's approach to this peculiarly self-policing, self-delighting, all-too-frequently-self-supporting profession. They are up on my wall, next to a list someone else has sent me on which everything is crossed out except the last item: *Sex. Drugs. Alcohol. Tobacco. Rock Music. Socialism. Caffeine.*

So, with mug of high octane coffee in hand, I pass them on. They are:

> *Show up.*
> *Pay attention.*
> *Tell the truth.*
> *Don't be attached to results.*

Some of those, believe me, are harder than they look.

Show up. This is the first, and possibly the most important, thing that separates the real writer from that glibly smiling face one encounters endlessly at parties who says, "One of these days when I get some spare time I'm going to write that book." He has (wittingly or with unacknowledged contempt) kicked sand in the writer's face with the implication that anyone can do it after the truly important things are off the desk. But he will not, as it happens, have the last laugh, because he will not accomplish that book by standing around drink in hand, saying it, planning it, and prematurely totting up the advance he's sure he'll nail down.

Showing up means sitting down pen in hand or fingers on keys. Not everyone can keep a regular schedule or even benefit by one. Just yesterday I spoke with a fairly prolific novelist who told me she lets her mind lie fallow for long periods, "just puttering, doing family things." People are made differently, and they receive or coerce their ideas in unpredictable rhythms. But the fact is that most productive writers show up for work as dutifully and with as little fanfare as any civil servant, and, of all of them, novelists tend to log hours that would strain the overtime budget of a small corporation.

I myself have attended, perhaps by now even graduated from, the William Stafford school of writing as he set it forth in his famous essay "On Writing." Stafford speaks of simply sitting down day in, day out, in a state of receptivity, and opening his mind so that whatever is swimming by will have a chance to swim *in*. Waiting for "inspiration" is a bad habit engendered, I think, by all we heard in college about Shelley and Coleridge slipping still-moist poems under each other's morning tea-cups after a night spent wrestling with the Divine Afflatus. Add to that the mistaken impression that "true artists" spend a lot of time drinking together or driving around the country in a Day-Glo painted bus or . . . The prototypes of the Bohemian are legion and they always seem to favor laziness or at least laxity where worktime is concerned. The fact is that every (visual) artist I know runs a mom and pop store in his or her studio that hardly ever closes; ditto the writers who actually get anything done. They are on call, in their places, at attention. And since they can't stand to be idle, once having shown up they will produce something, even if they think they're only waiting for a really good idea to walk in. (Whereupon William Stafford's second famous dictum kicks in: He did not, he said, believe in writer's block. Said Mr. Stafford, "I just lower my standards.")

My addendum to *Show up:* Probably the most important thing I've learned, after the fragmented years of child-raising were past (and even then I did my best and usually succeeded) was to arrange my available time in order of "quality" (as one does, in fact, with children). I asked myself which were my best hours for concentration, which less useful, which the dispensable ones when I could do all the things that don't take purity of attention. This seems self-evident but it is not. If you order your time this way, you don't clean up the house first thing in the morning, as an astonishing number of women do; you fit it in when you've got your pages done. (I've heard audiences gasp when I've said that nobody cares when the bed is made and the breakfast dishes done as long as they get done sometime, and not necessarily by *you*.) You don't do lunch. You don't attend noontime lectures. In the end, in fact, you renounce a lot of minor pleasures. (There are analogies to economic choices here—a lot of things that don't feel like choices but necessities are in fact within your control, if you choose to exercise it. As a confirmed connoisseur of thrift shops, I am often shocked to discover where my graduate students shop. If they're in for the long haul, Macy's can be a dangerous habit.) Much of the time such discipline feels indefensibly rigid; with tedious regularity I've had to apologize to others and to myself for being such a stick-in-the-mud. But when people say "Whoo, you've published nine books; you've raised children; you've taught. Wow, how'd you manage to do that?" I can only reply, with whatever misgivings, "I said no a lot."

And a second addendum: One of the benefits, not inconsiderable, of being what Tillie Olsen has called (rather poignantly, I think, because its effects so frequently eluded her) "an *habituated* writer," is the respect your habit elicits from those who would otherwise dismiss your work as hobby. John Cheever, it is said, put on a suit and tie every morning when he lived in Manhattan and went down in the elevator with the office workers in his building, then ducked into the laundry room where he removed his uniform and got to work. (I'm not sure I believe that but it makes a hell of a story.) I've never bought a little gray suit to go out in, or hidden pen and notebook in my briefcase, but I'll say for myself that my own need for vocation—for my work to be taken as seriously as any lawyer's or scientist's—has made a very necessary space in the minds of others. Spouses, lovers, friends, family, all of them will respect your time, your need for concentration, your seriousness only if you dare to respect it yourself. The room of your own may or may not have actual walls but the emotional space is yours to create and make absolutely clear; the world will flow in like a river to wash it away unless you protect it. And everything's easier than the double commitment that comes with *showing up,* everything: saying "I'm not here, I'm somewhere else. Ignore me." And then sitting down and doing it, disappearing into the work. Being there.

Pay attention. "Be someone on whom nothing is lost": one of Henry James's most fruitful utterances. A lovely instruction because it implicates the whole body, the whole soul. It reminds us that a writer lives in a state almost as magical as pregnancy, in which everything ingested is threshed into useful nourishment. Nothing is irrelevant, there is nothing that is not worth learning. Imagine, curiosity as part of your job description! Walker Evans, the great photographer, said it with bracing directness: "Stare. It is the only way to educate your eye, and more. Stare, pry, listen, eavesdrop. Die knowing something. You are not here long."

Item: I had a friend once, a literary journalist and critic, who thought it a waste of time to read the newspaper. "Why spend time on all that ephemera?" she asked me. "Anything important will make itself evident eventually, and everything unimportant deserves to drop away." It was during the same conversation that she happened to ask me how I knew some of the things I wrote about in my novel *The Autobiography of My Mother.* "By reading the newspaper," I told her. I read the *New York Times* from the back, starting with the "trivial" stories.

Item: My most recent novel, *Before and After,* was stimulated by something that was all over the Houston papers for months when I lived there. I do not remember paying much attention to it. But four years after it happened, when I wanted to write a play I remembered the headlines. Had I registered them subliminally? Why did they surface so much later? Presumably I had things on my mind that could finally come together with those events, but they were emotional, not factual, matters. How do we know when our oblique glance is hitting the very object we need? Of course we don't. But the more we've seen, read, *registered,* the greater the likelihood. And those connections are the most interesting moment— no, second, like the *ffft!* of a match—in the process of writing.

Another addendum: And beyond the *New York Times* lies the world, the real, not the reflected, one. If you're paying attention, this entirely honorable conflict will so often emerge: Do I stay home writing, protecting my time and my psyche as if they were violinist's hands, or do I leave my study (my carrel, my corner of the bedroom) and go out into the time-consuming, energy-devouring world of action and social usefulness and leave the writing in a neglected heap? This is a hard dilemma. We all decide where our best talents lie. Somewhere along the way, when I lived in Mississippi in the mid-60s and stayed home and wrote about what I saw, I made the guilt-wracked decision that I was less effective on the barricades than I was at capturing some internal record of the costs of the life I saw around me. When my book of poems was published, one generous reviewer exonerated me by saying "Poems are an event too." But then there is Grace Paley, touchstone to the side of me that stays sorry: she has written little but brilliantly, she has made useful matter of the political struggle she's perennially engaged in, and she's been a good citizen of the world. ("Noble" is a word Grace won't allow.) No one can choose for you. As the old sad civil rights song (probably derived from a hymn) says it, "You've got to do it / for yourself."

Tell the truth. Well, now, there's an easy one. This little shard of advice is so huge, so deep, so difficult, that its appearance on that list feels a little disingenuous. It is the elementary challenge every writer picks up unless he or she intends to be a pop star and tell the falsehoods so many readers love to hear.

But, in spite of intentions, to some extent we are helpless before our habits and capacities: It is our characters (our own moral substance, I mean, not the people we create on paper) that must answer for it. What in fact does it mean to tell the truth in our writing? We are only as complex as we are—but we ought not allow ourselves to be less complex in our work than in our lives, no matter how commercially inconvenient that might sometimes be, or how it compromises the chance to humiliate the characters we don't like (this time I mean the written ones). That, I suppose, is one kind of truth. Do we say everything we know (or imagine) about someone, even if the someone is our own creation? How do we know when to use a fist and when a gloved hand? What is compassion and what is sentimentality? When are we being a shade too ingratiating and when needlessly sensational, going for the blurb that will call our book "relentless, uncompromising"? How do we learn to trust ourselves to know?

I once read a horrifying list (I remember, though perhaps imperfectly, that it was Edward Hoagland's) of the character weaknesses to be found in writers, that were, not surprisingly, duplicated in their work. It read like a psychiatrist's notes on the patient before treatment. *An incapacity for love. An inability to come to terms with the opposite sex. A tin ear for suffering. An overfastidious distaste for children. A fear of getting to know people. An autodidact's smugness or an Ivy League snobbery. The vice of perennial experimentation. A weakness for enlisting himself in every flibberty new vogue or cause.* Do those accusations, if such they are, affect our capacity to be truthful in our writing (not to mention our *lives*)? Not purposely, but surely they do. They are our excuses for lying; they are our own intimate failures. I have no answers to the questions they raise except to suggest that we cultivate humility in their presence. *Absence of humility,* in fact, would be my own addition to the list, a deficiency so common to writers who need sufficient confidence to persist in the face of every kind of indifference that they cannot always find the balance between courage and arrogance. It would be an interesting challenge to add your own least favorite sins, and then narrow your eyes next time you read your own work. . . .

And finally: *Don't be attached to results.*

After a while, of course, this list makes one into a Freshman Comp. teacher. I want to say, define your terms! Whose definition of results? One's own? One's best (but most honest) critic? The publishing powers? The public? How can one not care? What separates caring about good work from caring about good press?

I will say, for myself, that while I am a decent critic of a word or a line of my own, I have little faith in my capacity to judge the whole, at least until a great deal of time goes by and possibly not even then: I'm quite capable of deriding my best work or reading in dumb awe something I knew or had the stamina to write that I didn't know I knew (which is on the same rudimentary level as admiring an actor for learning his lines). But often, to be shamefully honest, I sometimes think that your capacity to judge the quality of your work is like trying to see the back of your head without a mirror.

Though readings are a wonderful antidote to the isolation in which you write, you can't trust audiences to give a finely nuanced hearing to your work—you are there, alive before them, and they are eager to like you. You can tell by the sound of their coughing and their shuffling feet whether, at the simplest level, they're engaged by what you're reading, but you know, you've been there—it all rushes by too fast for trustworthy judgment. And not all good writing makes good listening. You may not want to amass one of those endless lists of thankable friends with which so many books begin today, but there is someone among everyone's friends, family, colleagues, who—given a general sympathy with one's sensibility—knows how to be harsh when necessary. Being an uncritical admirer is as easy as it is useless.

As for the reception of the work by strangers—the commercial life of the work—since I have already quoted my betters, here is one more: Kipling, who must have known whereof he spoke, said *Beware the twin imposters, success and failure.* I believe he was saying, in his way, *Don't be attached to results.* The poem, the story, the novel in the hand, they succeed or fail on their own terms, by being fully what they intended to be or not—and ultimately what they wanted to be, how large, how challenging, how original, will be judged as well. Whether they sell—and if you write books, how well they sell—is so little correlated (if not inversely correlated) with quality that in the end it is only your sense of satisfaction that will define your success. The standards of the market are cruel and, worse, irrelevant to the internal pleasure (and the minor perks) of the writing life. There have been nights when, skepticism aside, reading to an audience has been quite enough for me. When, re-reading, I've said "Yes, that's what I wanted, just that." Eudora Welty says we write for the "it." No one can define that interaction of need and fulfillment. When you find the word, when you hit the rhythm—I hang a good sentence or paragraph over my workplace so that I can try to hit it again—isn't it like dancing? Like music? Like the sound of the bat connecting or the basket giving off its little vibrating "zing" when the ball drops through? Those are results, though they may not be bankable.

"Success" and "failure," those big nouns that summarize our accomplishments as though to determine whether we should live or die, are adjudicated in public by people who do not much care about us personally, let alone how we feel as we work. If you have a career, it will (let's assume) be a long one, and nothing—not love or marriage or friendship, not health, not energy—exists over time without peaks and pits and flatland in between. Everything you write fits into that larger landscape: today's "failed" piece may be the nub of tomorrow's newly conceived "success." Tomorrow's "success" may be toxic for your psychic life. One of my happiest moments came when I discovered that I knew how to swallow a "failure" and not be undone by it; had the work "succeeded," I'm not sure what, if anything, I would have learned about myself.

In the end, for me it's simply this: The only way we really ought to let those judgments touch us—after listening hard for what resonates with our own deepest estimate of what we've done—is to take from them the correction or the confidence or the hunger to write another day without fearing that the gods are laughing.

Janet Burroway

Janet Burroway is the author of plays, poetry, children's books, and seven novels, including *The Buzzards, Raw Silk, Opening Nights,* and, most recently, *Cutting Stone.* She writes a regular essay column for *New Letters* magazine and frequently reviews for the *New York Times Book Review.* Her text *Writing Fiction* is used in more than three hundred colleges and universities in the United States. Her play *Medea with Child,* recipient of the 1997 Reva Shiner Prize, was produced by the Bloomington Playwrights' Project; her novel *Opening Nights* was adapted for National Public Radio. She is Robert O. Lawton Distinguished Professor at Florida State University.

How to stare one of our occupational hazards, the monster Envy, in its fearful eye and win back our self-esteem.

Re: Envy

Dear D——

Rec'd your *cri de coeur* (dead of winter, dead of night) and return you a hug and a mug of hot cocoa (*not* toddy) which I am sorry you will have to administer yourself. Yes, I had heard of both the prize and the advance. C.K. is a terrier with the rat reputation in his teeth, and R.M. has parlayed a flea's output into an elephant's feast and yes you are suffering envy and yes your outcry is justified and yes it is corrosive.

And yes I'll tell you what I know about envy. Your request means that I should impart some wisdom, but by way of credential let me tell you what I *know* about envy. It begins as you describe, with some fact overheard or learned in conversation, announced in a letter or a newsletter or the back pages of *Poets and Writers* or arts section of the *NY Times* or the cover of *People*. It involves someone with whom you have a connection, personal or institutional or aesthetic, intimate or tenuous, new or ongoing or, God forbid, *over.* It records a grant, a prize, a publication, an amount of money, kudos, a command performance. Though it is probably not unlike some such announcement made about yourself at some point in the not truly distant past, nevertheless it has a gloss and glory that is, for you, unattainable or lost and never to be or never again to be achieved. The fact, whatever it may be, registers as a small spasm in the stomach or the throat, followed by an exudation of bile as thin as whey that runs sour through the bloodstream to the crown, soles, fingernails, which may make crescents in the underbelly of your hands, though against whom or what you are fisted you don't exactly know. The sensation is akin to rejection but is different from rejection, which makes you a victim whereas envy also makes you a villain. This is why it is so itchy, such a little-ease. You dislike it because it reveals your bad self to you. Do I know?

The thing I know about envy is that it comes and goes. It doesn't come because you're unregarded and it doesn't go because you're swathed in glitz. On the contrary, I suspect it gets keener as you rise, as you discover that the first reward of celebrity is an unlisted number, and that just because somebody wants to touch the hem of your garment does not necessarily mean he's read your *book*. I remember one week-end in London, when a novelist friend (whom I won't betray by naming) had to babysit with one of the most powerful actresses in Hollywood, a woman whose fortune and fame are right out of the range of our desire, famous beyond the Nobel winners and rich beyond the Bulls—who spent the weekend dissolved in tears because she was not *this* year nominated for an Oscar. On the other hand my new advisee Leslie bounced into the office last week, having acquired both a jaw and *posture,* ready to take on the world, because she'd got an A in Freshman Comp. You and I both are in the world-ly middle between these two, and all I can tell you for sure is that your skills and your resume will grow; but as for envy, it comes and goes.

If I think about it clearly, I suspect that what *I* envy is something that does not exist, that I have made up out of my own struggles, the illusion that this shining reward, whatever it is, came to whoever it came to out of the blue, and that she/he plucked it bright-feathered out of the air, with none of the gnashing and moiling, the self-disgust and petty despairs that I went through. Which is dim. And disses not the win-ning but the struggle. Lit. history is littered with Richard Cory's. How envied little Tommy Chatterton must have been!

and Papa Hemingway, and Virginia Woolf; and I was close enough to Sylvia Plath myself to smart at her dazzle; and, so recently it takes the breath, thought Michael Dorris had a charmed and charming life.

All the deadly sins have a virtue on the flip side—as, the virtue of pride is self-esteem, the virtue of gluttony is appetite, the virtue of sloth is ease and so forth. A. S. Byatt pointed out in the *NYTBR* a few years ago that the virtue of envy is justice, the impulse a primal, "It's not *fair!*" And you and I know there's not a lot of *fair* in the space between art and fame. There's not *no* justice, that'd be far too easy. There's a little. It's Beckett's universe, where you couldn't claim that things make no sense at all, but that they promise a meaning and then thwart you of it. So with just rewards in art. Some are adulated who deserve it, and some come to their reward in time, some are honored but kept poor, and some get rich but scorned, as befits them. But only some, and only sometimes. Just as often the shallow are revered, the brilliant go unnoticed.

Right now we know this injustice is severe; the arts are on the outs in our money-run society; it's harder and harder to find a soul with any *summum bonum* but the bottom line. We blame the times, but these are the only times we have, and the knowledge of our wrongs makes us more petulant than revolutionary. Anyway, writers have always been mad for fame, there is no news in that, nothing that can be set exclusively at the feet of the corporate world; and the desire to write is distributed with an intensity that bears no relation whatsoever to the talent attached. Awful writers and mediocre writers use exactly the same reasoning as the righteous—that editors want only blockbusters, that reviewers are showing off. You've known writers who had no conversation except their agents' fees and how Hollywood has no brain. Ho hum. No literature was ever made out of these impulses— Louise Bogan used to claim that you can make poetry out of hatred but not *spite*—although as subject matter they have given us Iago, *The Changeling, The Information, Amadeus.*

Othello's problem is a different sort, but what a writer's envy has in common with sexual jealousy is that it can eat away at reason and bring about the very thing it fears. Nobody can write well who is thinking about somebody else's unjust deserts. So for as long as envy holds us, we twist in a space that allows no stretch. That feeling—mortification at another's prosperity—has as its natural inverse *Schadenfreude,* pleasure at another's misfortune. And that of course is next door to cruelty, pleasure in another's pain. Yet envy stings the one who feels it, and, so little injures the one at whom it is aimed, that if he or she should learn of it, she/he would react with sour delight.

It strikes me too that envy has the same nature as revenge, the way Greeks and the Renaissance tragedians understood it, how it proceeds from justice to corruption. The Greeks acknowledged as a divine law that the murderer must pay by being murdered, the only trouble being that the avenger was certain to be corrupted by his vengeance. So then he must be punished, and so forth. Aeschylus understood that the only way to break this murderous chain was to act from a pure heart. Then Shakespeare and Webster pointed out how hard it is to keep the heart from rotting. Look how our feelings for the Duchess of Malfi turn from sympathy to flinching ambivalence. She's surrounded by corruption and we want her to win free, but in order to do so she must lie, and lie again, and then be trapped in a lie and then trapped by a lie, and the lies become more blatant, blasphemous, bloodier.

Virginia Woolf registered the ambivalence—it is more than that, an emotional oxymoron—in her journal of 28 Nov. '28, when Lytton Strachey's *Elizabeth and Essex* was about to come out:

> I kept thinking: well, if he can palm that off on us after years of effort—that lively superficial meritricious book . . . And although one of my vile vices is jealousy, of other writers' fame, though I am (& think we all are) secretly pleased to find Lytton's book a bad one, I also feel depressed. If I were to analyse, the truth is I think that the pleasure is mean, & therefore not deep or satisfying; one would, in the depths, have got real pleasure, though superficial pain, had E&E been a masterpiece. Oh yes, I should.
> . . . for I have a mind that feeds perfectly dispassionately & apart from my vanities & jealousies upon literature; and that would have taken a masterpiece to itself.

What she has caught is the truth that there are two kinds of envy. One is the desire for the rewards, contains a mean-spirited judgment, gives rise to *Schadenfreude*. The other is envy of the talent and the accomplishment, and it enfolds admiration, it has the force of inspiration: oh, if only I could produce something as wonderful as this image, this line, this book by Margaret Atwood, Doris Lessing, Don DeLillo, George Eliot (one good, perhaps not flawless, test is whether you would still envy the person if she/he were dead).

And this envy has its uses. It is a sign of life—if you think that's disingenuous, you haven't been clinically depressed. There is a kind of bitter dull acceptance of the world's injustice, a desolate welcome to it, to feel which might make you envy the envious.

More, it can teach you what you want, and therefore where

to put your effort; in French the verb *envier* is *to envy* but the noun *envie* is *desire*. For instance, do you now or did you ever envy Pol Pot? Donald Trump? Monica Lewinsky? See? If not, is it really power or money or the spotlight that you crave? If so, mebbe you should consider getting out, because the chances of publishing your way to it are about the same as the Publishers' Clearinghouse sweepstakes. But I think it isn't the reward you want, but the deserving of it, because I've watched you work a story to its own triumph, and because if the joy is not in the work, there's not payoff enough in the world to keep either you or me in place for all these hours.

The real rewards are the idea that makes a gift of itself, and the moment it seems to be netted onto the page. The only fame that counts is the moment we won't share, with someone we'll never know, when that idea hits home. All you can do with the energy of envy is to take it back to work. And I will envy you without rancor, Dear D, if you will please get back to that book and get it out in the world.

Raymond Carver

Raymond Carver (1938–1988) is an exemplary artist of the short form, writing honest and apparently plain stories that are triumphs of hidden artistry. In his work, collected in *Where I'm Calling From,* we find Hemingway's rhythms and ability to suggest, while not directly talking about, great pain; Chekhov, too, is alive in Carver's stories—the grappling with appetite, the wish to be simple, the need to address the darkness.

Carver's great decency and generosity are evident in this letter as he addresses alcoholism, which has been called the writer's disease.

Dear Mr. Hallstrom

September 17, 1986

Dear Mr. Hallstrom

Thanks for your good letter. I was away from here for a few days or else you would have had a reply from me before now.

Well, as you say, everyone's recovery is different, but it took me at least six months—more—after I stopped drinking before I could attempt to do any more than write a few letters. Mainly I was so grateful to have my health back, and my life back, that it really didn't matter to me in one large way if I ever wrote anything again, or not. I wrote just a little bit, a story or two, if that, between six months and eight or ten months after getting sober. Again, I must say I didn't worry about it, in the largest sense. I remember feeling that it was quite possible that I might never write anything "creative" again, and that was all right, too, somehow. Finally, my letter writing paid off, and I landed a one-year job teaching at the U of Texas at El Paso. This would have been for the academic year 1978–1979. Fact, I'd been sober for well over a year and I still wasn't writing, but I tell you, and it's true, I wasn't worrying about it. I was just very happy, very happy to be alive. Then, in El Paso, I wrote a few poems and began to do a few book reviews (I was asked to do them and I was pleased to be able to do them) for the *Chicago Tribune*. I don't think I began to write seriously until the fall of 1979, when Tess and I were living in Tucson, where she was teaching at the time (I'd somehow been given a Guggenheim Fellowship, and I had that, and a job to look forward to at Syracuse); and pretty soon that fall I started working on a story and finished it, and then began another one, and then another one. So, with the exception of a few book reviews, and a very few poems, after the first year of sobriety (and almost nothing the first year), it took me two years, a bit more than two years, to get into the swing of things again. I didn't know if I could do it again or not. It came, yes, but it came very, very slowly for the longest while after getting sober. Jesus, the whole drinking thing is such an ordeal and so much time and effort go into that, and your thinking is so fucked and your brains scrambled, it just takes the longest while to ever get on track again. But it'll come. Use this time of not writing to just get acquainted with yourself again, and do lots of reading and re-reading, the things that mattered so long ago when you were young and innocent, read those things over again. And go to AA meetings if it's necessary; and it was necessary for me for the longest while—six or eight months or so; and I've gone a number of times too since then, taking friends who wanted to go. But I don't think you should feel too anxious about the present situation. I mean, you just don't need any more than the usual anxiety right now, the anxieties we all walk around with, they're quite enough to deal with during this recovery period. Don't worry, try not to worry, about whether or not you will ever write again, or if you've wasted your life, or the better part of your life, by staying soused all the time. For the first month or so after getting sober, maybe two months, I felt absolutely crazy, nearly, every morning I woke up. I mean I felt great in one way, that I knew I was waking up sober, but I felt I'd pissed away years and years that I'd never get back; and felt, too, like I hadn't done any work at all and that what I had done wasn't worth anything, etc. It's just that you're trying to put a life together, trying to make something out of just about nothing. It's starting over, and in a big way. . . . And I wasn't able to write toward the end of my drinking career, either. I hardly wrote anything at all for the last two years of my drinking. So, add that to the long time it took me after getting sober, and you can see just where I was. Nowhere, but I was sober, and that was everything.

It'll come, you'll see. In its own good time, it'll come. Incidentally, I had a long conversation about this with the late Dick Hugo. He told me pretty much the same thing. The last years of his drinking, he was only writing one or two poems a year. And it took him a long while to get going again after he'd stopped.

Listen, I'm glad you wrote to me. I'm sorry if this seems hasty, or not very considered and thoughtful, but I wanted to get some kind of response back to you before any more time had elapsed.

Stay well. Don't drink, as they say. Think of me if ever you feel like you want to drink. I know if I can kick it, well, then there is hope for just about anybody. I had the world's worst case of it.

Write me again in a month or two, or whenever it's right, and tell me how you are and what you're doing.

This is with every good wish.

Warmly,
Ray Carver

✦

Malcolm Cowley

He was a poet in Europe with the Lost Generation and he chronicled their adventures in *Exiles' Return*. Famous as the literary editor of the *New Republic,* he was an important editor at Viking, instituting the Viking Portable Library series; he is responsible for the *Portable Faulkner,* which, in 1946, resurrected Faulkner's reputation (two of his seventeen books were in print). He corresponded with, and was extraordinarily helpful to, such writers as Jack Kerouac, Ernest J. Gaines, and Tillie Olsen.

The subject of this letter is not only John Cheever's great story "Goodbye, My Brother," but cant, jargon, and straight talk.

Letter to John Cheever

Sherman, Conn.
February 11, 1953

Dear John:

I wish you'd tell me more about Goodbye, My Brother. Not about what you call your failure in it, but about what you intended to do, because I certainly missed that and I don't even get it completely clear from the recent explanation. As I see it now Lawrence was a real person, actually lived and all that, but his dark interpretation of his family's motives was read into him by the story-telling brother, who really had those dark interpretations himself, underneath, and who tried to kill Lawrence in order to kill the rebellion in himself. Then the dark head and the golden head rise out of the water to symbolize the two sides of his nature—but how the hell do they make the story any less ambiguous? And is this the right Meaning after all?

I'm getting bothered not only about this story but about a whole trend in current fiction, the one represented by "meanings on several different levels," that phrase one finds among the critical comments by Eudora Welty et al. printed on the back of the dust wrapper of all the New Fiction titles, under the cabinet-size photograph of the author with his finely shaped artist's hand resting lightly on his cheek and an intent, other-worldly look around his eyes. "Meanings on several different levels" wasn't in the beginning but is getting to be a lot of shit. The bright boys at Princeton keep asking their instructor, "What does a story mean?"—by which *they* mean, What is its inner or anagogic or cabalistic meaning? They forget that it has to be a story first, that if an object isn't real in the beginning it is worthless as a symbol, that if a character isn't real he isn't an archetype of reality, that if an event isn't real it can't be a myth.

I thought, when I read Goodbye, My Brother that it was a fine story, that all the characters except Lawrence were very solid, that the two women rising out of the sea were a fine image in themselves, and I didn't care what they Meant. My trouble was the fundamental ambiguity: Lawrence's criticisms of the family's life were partly justified, but Lawrence was a heel and didn't have the right to make the criticisms, so that I didn't know where the author stood, or whether he was being fashionably Aloof and Ironic and Ambiguous (which has come to be a term of praise). (Which also has become a justification for the author's not having made up his mind, not being Engaged—another dreadful cliché—not ever wanting to say, this is good, this is bad.) Maybe my trouble is that you were too much of a writer to make Lawrence a figment and hallucination—he was too real for that without being real enough.

But for all this fault it's a fine story and brings me back to that point I made—when you write a novel it will have to start with a story like this and grow backward, explain, clarify the people, instead of starting with a big, complicated plot that will keep breaking down into episodes and short set pieces.

. . .

As ever,

Nicholas Delbanco

Nicholas Delbanco has published seventeen books of fiction and nonfiction. His first novel, *The Martlet's Tale,* appeared in 1966, his most recent, *Old Scores,* in 1997. Founding Director of the Bennington Writing Workshops, he has served as Chair of the Hopwood Awards Program at the University of Michigan, where he has been a Professor of English since 1985.

A meditation on a life in art, and upon the inspiration for this book, Rilke's Letters to a Young Poet.

Dear Franz K

Dear Franz K:

You don't exist. Well, all right, you did exist but your last name's not Kafka and very few remember you except as a recipient or, as your teacher might have said, a *receptacle,* a *vessel.* Rainer Maria Rilke wrote letters to you long ago, and they are what we have. You are and were the young poet— strange convention of critical discourse, that we employ the present tense—to whom he dispensed and dispenses advice. "The blue-sealed letter bore the postmark of Paris, weighed heavy in the hand, and showed on the envelope the same beautiful, clear, sure characters in which the text was set down from the first line to the last . . ." That's what you wrote, remembering, from *Berlin, June, 1929.*

That the letters should remain in print is no small credit to your powers of attention and retention; you do survive as witness and conservator, Herr K., and for this you have our thanks. Thanks also for the modesty with which you excised your own missives to him, the ones that he so scrupulously answered but have been long since lost. *Letters to a Young Poet* fails to amount to a shared correspondence, replicating turn by turn the letters *from* . . .

Or perhaps you kept no copies of the lines you wrote, and probably he didn't bother to preserve them; you were neither rich, female, nor famous. Too, he traveled a good deal those years, and no doubt he thought—who can blame him?—that he'd discharged his debt to you by writing and tore your letters in two. Then the great man let your stationery flutter to the floor for servants to collect, or balled the fragments up and tossed them into the fireplace negligently, or left them behind in the hotel or guest-room escritoire when he traveled on. At any rate, my friend, the conversation was one-sided— an interrupted monologue—and you'll forgive me if I follow where he led. He *used* you, Franz; he was ready to answer your questions and you furnished the occasion and after he expressed himself he dropped off your personal map.

So too will I. These lines are a "one-off," a variation on a theme, and I want to use you—to quote another poet of a slightly later era—in order to mix those paired ingredients, "memory and desire." I've been teaching now for a very long time, have produced unnumbered thousands of pages in response to student writing, and since I remember what it meant to read such letters early on I take this chance as a high charge: I want to tell you what I can about the world of words . . .

And yet the topic daunts. Not so much the topic, perhaps, as our collective title—with its tipped cap to Rainer Maria Rilke and the otherwise-forgotten Franz Xaver Kappus. You who sat on a park bench in 1902, with a book by Rilke on your lap, and were moved to write him and engender a response. Like that person from Porlock who interrupted Coleridge in the dear dream of "Kubla Khan," Herr Kappus deserves a foot-note in literary history; without you we'd not have this record of advice. You both went to school at the Military Academy in Wiener-Neustadt, and neither of you liked the military life; your letter touched a nerve. Not all that hard to do with Rilke, let's admit; he was neurasthenic to a fault, and ready as a tun-ing fork to vibrate when properly struck.

But the "young poet" must have been astonished; he sent off some apprentice verse and reaped a returning whirlwind from Paris, then Viareggio, then Worpswede, Sweden and Rome. There are ten of these epistles; they span the years from 1903 to 1908. The first of them is dated five years short of a century ago: *Paris, February 17th, 1903.* Sometimes hectoring, often runic, always generous, the pages set a standard it's not easy now to meet: Rilke wrote with a sense of his own consideration and a high grave consequence, one eye fixed upon eternity and one eye on the clock . . .

So yes, my dear Kappus, I swallowed you whole. I was trying to learn German, and the M. D. Herter Norton translation served admirably as trot. The letters gave an early clue as to what it might entail to make of writing a profession. I had been given a copy of *Briefe an einen jungen Dichter* by an uncle who well understood I hoped to be a writer; he himself had translated Rilke from his own *muttersprache* in order to improve his sense of the English language and the diction to which, courtesy of Adolf Hitler, he had been as an adult consigned. My uncle knew great swatches of the *Duino Elegies* by heart, and he would nod approvingly while I recited too. Once when I offered up, from Rilke's *Notebooks of Malte Laurids Brigge,* the defining phrase: *"Er war ein Dichter, das heisst, er hasste das Ungefähr,"* my uncle asked, "But how would you apply it?"

" 'He was a poet,' " I translated. " 'Which is to say, he despised the approximate.' Or perhaps, 'hated the inexact.' "

"Not bad," he said. "Not bad . . ."

I was a senior in college. My thesis dealt in part with Rilke's *Neue Gedichte,* and everything about the man compelled me: his intricate affairs, his picturesque quasi-poverty, his time with the sculptor Auguste Rodin, his passive-aggressive familiarity with aristocrats, preferably female, his series of patrons, his prose, his energetic listless pose, his verse. How splendid it would be, I thought, to wander the world making sonnets and sit in lamplit circles sipping wine from crystal goblets while, somewhere, a lutenist strummed. I dreamed of full-skirted consorts on the beach near Bremen and read the biography of Lou Andreas-Salome with near-prurient delight. Oh, Rilke was my Yeats. The castle walls, the words from the wind, the stagey stages of a career and death of a rare blood disease—pricked by a rose-bush, he failed to recover—all these were just the thing. *Das Ding an sich,* the thing itself, the *thingsomeness,* the *thingliness,* would furnish my aesthetic as it had structured his. Even his early and pretentious rhyme (who really reads the *Erste* and *Frühe Gedichte*?) then struck me as good news, a sign that one could get better by *willing* it, that a sense of vocation sufficed.

By now I'm not so sure. The poet's eyes that seemed so luminous with pain and bliss in the old photographs strike me, today, as watery, and the moustache droops. Rilke was only twenty-seven when he began to write to Kappus, and much of the elder young poet's advice looks inward-facing merely: Narcissus in the mirror if not pool. The roses and the maidens and the lighthouses and Orphic utterances—"The love which consists in this: that two solitudes protect and limit and greet each other"—now seem a little humid to me, and poor long-suffering Clara Rilke put up with a good deal. His characteristic *Leben Sie wohl!*—the "Live Well" with which RMR concludes a letter—is often as not self-serving or at least self-dramatizing; why bother to harangue poor Kappus, insisting that, like some sort of cobbler, he needed to stick to his last?

Whatever the motive, and whether causal or coincidental, the effect of Rilke's hortatory instruction was that his pupil ceased to write: ". . . life drove me off," Kappus later admitted, "into those very regions from which the poet's warm, tender and touching concern had sought to keep me." Well, perhaps . . .

But it's unkind to satirize the sacred texts of one's own youth or to reclassify those sacred cows as bull. Like *The Prophet* or *Siddhartha,* the *Letters to a Young Poet* are a young person's book. I can't read them now with the wide-eyed wonder that obtained when I first found the volume; there's too much heavy oracular breathing and faith in the privileged self. Too small a proportion of the ten letters deals with the work at hand, too much with the as-yet-unwritten ideal; my own best notion of how to help students has more to do with close reading and "the thing itself."

Still, these are talismanic texts: Franz Kappus tapped a golden vein and Rilke's mine was rich. And the great line at the end of the great poem about the archaic torso of Apollo rings as true to me today as it did when I first read it more than thirty years ago. It remains a clarion call for the young fiction writer as well as to the poet: *Du musst dein Leben ändern.* "You must change your life."

This season I've learned two new lessons about what might as well be called the writing life. My own has had a disconcerting longevity by now; though I think of myself as a schoolboy with his satchel and shining morning face, I'm someone who published his first novel more than thirty years ago and should probably wear trifocals. It's been a longish haul. So it's not perhaps surprising that the landscape alters or that there be milestones in a marathon—but these two do look like markers to describe.

The first is wholly happy and a cause for celebration. In 1984 I was teaching in a workshop, the Bread Loaf Writers'

Conference in Middlebury, Vermont. This is a place where tuition-paying amateurs show their work to putative profession- als in the hope of affirmation; in theatrical terms it's the equiv- alent of an open casting call. Each of the staff members was assigned some twenty or so such hopefuls; they'd been told to provide us with manuscripts and then foregather in class.

One of the works, I remember, was a pearl among white peas. The story was called "The Apple Picker Hits the Road," and it seemed letter-perfect to me then, and it does so still. Its author turned out to be a silent, lanky, nervous young woman in the corner of the room; she had not shown her work or received encouragement before. I next asked to see the novel she confessed to have been working on for years. It was full of amateur errors, and I said so, and that seemed to establish some trust between us; she'd been wary of what she took to be unfounded praise but responded with real interest to a sustained critique.

So we remained in touch; we wrote letters and saw each other intermittently; when the time came I invited her to give readings here in Ann Arbor and teach in the graduate writing program for which I served as Director; over the last ten years or so I've watched her shelf of books increase with something very like paternal pride. Her name is Andrea Barrett; her most recent effort, a splendid collection of interlocked tales called *Ship Fever & Other Stories* received the National Book Award for fiction in 1996. To return to my opening trope, if a career may be described as race I've had the chance to watch Ms. Barrett in a starter's crouch and hit her stride and break the tape; she has, as it were, breathtakingly arrived.

That "pride" alluded to above is, I believe, characteristic. Take any group of writers and sooner or later they'll tell you who they worked with when, who taught them what or whom they taught. And though some of this may sound like profit-sharing or mere boastfulness, it is on the whole benign. Every teacher worth the name takes pleasure in the success of students, and the more the merrier; to believe that the victory of X must necessarily entail the defeat of Y or Z is, I think, absurd. We have labored far too long with the imagery of Oscar night and the misleading metaphor of prize-fights; art can claim no "heavyweight champ" or "knockout performance" or lone contender left in the ring; a large book enlarges us all.

I have carried with me for some time the notion of writers as artisans: artists engaged in a guild. The model is that of the medieval cadre, with its compelling triad of apprentice, then journeyman laborer, then master-craftsman—this last attained after a lifetime's study and practice of the craft. That writing is a craft as well as art, that one must learn to dado the paragraph's joinings, as it were, or prime the canvas of the scene—this is something we take increasingly for granted. But the stages of apprenticeship seem at the least confusing; it is not a mere matter of time. Who provides the walking papers; who does the training, the teaching; who ratifies our membership and says "Welcome to the guild . . ."?

There are several plausible candidates. There are agents, editors, publishers; there are critics and prize-giving committees; there are writing programs, hydra-headed lately, and writing conferences and workshops and festivals and an audience of strangers growing intimate as we whisper secrets—with the high hope that thousands will read them—we might hesitate to tell a family member or friend. There are professional contests to enter: the lottery called influence, the lottery called fame. There is inward certainty, discovery, the knowledge that we now can manage what we once could not. But surely one of the ways we know we are writers is when writers tell us so, pointing out a way through the dark wood . . .

Max Eastman was in his eighties when I was in my twenties. We met on Martha's Vineyard and grew close; he was tolerance incarnate, with an amused abiding sense of how youth preens. I postured; I was working on a book *(Grasse 3/23/66)* that was recondite in the extreme. I'd labor in an ecstasy of self-congratulation, producing perhaps a hundred words a day, intoning the sibylline syllables until they appeared to make sense. One such passage, I remember, contained a quotation from Villon, a description of Hopi burial rites, an anagram of the name of my fifth-grade teacher, an irrefutable refutation of Kant, glancing reference to Paracelsus, suggestive ditto to my agent's raven-haired assistant, paraphrase of Cymbeline's dirge, and an analysis of the orthographic and conceptual disjunction between Pope and Poe. I took my time; I let it extend to ten lines. That night I brought my morning's triumph to Max and permitted him to read. He did so in silence. He tried it aloud; so did I. When he said it made no sense and I explained the sense it made, he looked at me with generous exasperation. "Sure," he said. "That's interesting. Why don't you write it down?"

The second milestone is less pleasant to describe. More than twenty years ago (the summer of 1977) my late colleague at Bennington College, John Gardner, and I began a Summer Writing Workshop in a kind of conceptual opposition to the model of Bread Loaf itself. Instead of students bringing what they thought of as accomplished prose for a thumbs-up or down we planned to accept only those who wished to labor at their projects while enrolled. Revision was expected and new drafts encouraged; our sessions resembled not so much an audition as rehearsal, and we read—or so it seems to me in retrospect—a prodigious amount of language from young and middle-aged and elderly writers who emerged from year-long solitude to share what they'd produced . . .

We kept them in town for four weeks while great practitioners like John Cheever and Bernard Malamud dropped by to monitor progress; it was a heady time. Next year we repeated and expanded the venture, adding other genres (poetry, non-fiction) and offering a two-week option for those who could not stay the month. The notion took root and flower; by now it has flourished mightily and it's difficult to throw a rock in New England during the summer without hitting a writers' conference. For a decade the Bennington Writing Workshops proved wildly successful and over-subscribed; students wanted, for good and sufficient reason, to come and sit at the feet of those who came to teach, and I've named only the enduring dead because those living writers who joined us are legion and because the workshop too has died. There's too much competition and too little local motivation; my successors as directors of the program have turned their attention elsewhere; Rest in Peace.

This, then, is a Requiem for a Writers' Conference—for all those vivid days and nights, those years in which we ate and drank and smoked and argued and embraced the very stuff of poetry and prose, those summer parties on the lawn and children on the swingsets and classes full, it seemed, of consequence: the discovery of talent and the dear dream it might thrive.

The present volume's editor was part of that party also, crucial to it at the start. He too has taught for decades and would,

I think, agree with me that it's an honorable profession; the transmission of craft-tips such letters entail need not be over-rated but should not be dismissed. It's not nothing that we do. Time after time the flattery of imitation will alter and enlarge to emulation; then emulation in its turn becomes originality. We copy and we borrow (a descant here, a har-mony there) until our own voice issues as chorale. The regret-filled reward for a teacher—or so Dante suggests it might have been the case for Virgil—is that moment when the guide avers: I have brought you to this distant place and now can lead no further. Fare forward, voyager.

This last phrase—once again, according to that preternatu-rally aged young poet, T. S. Eliot—is the Buddha's dying vale-diction to his grief-stricken disciples: "Not farewell, but fare forward, voyager." And Eliot's notion of "Tradition and the Individual Talent" is also useful here. What we hope to teach our students is in some sense an echo of the texts we studied at some other someone's behest; the past stays current in the telling, and if I shamelessly refer to Dante and Virgil and Eliot, not to mention Gautama Buddha, it's because their music still sounds out to me in a way that makes all present song but variation on a theme. What we know of Dante's Florence or Virgil's Carthage, after all, comes down to us in language, and if you remember nothing else about this letter, Franz, remem-ber please to read . . .

Writing cannot, we are told, be taught; it must nonetheless be learned. How does one make sense of such a paradox, and one with which an increasing number of us live? It's easy to inveigh against the workshop "groupie" or the author who solicits opinion for the same manuscript time and again, then shifts a semicolon or excises an adjective and believes that this draft's a new draft. Not every teacher merits respectful attention and not every student improves. But the worst that's done is not much harm and the best is a good deal better than that; a culture does itself no damage by attending to its language, and often such a collocation can yield real results; the history of art is full of stories, strategies, techniques, and lessons exchanged.

"The best things come," as Henry James averred in his book about Hawthorne, "from the talents that are members of a group."

I have been the full-fledged student of a writer only once. John Updike is, I think, one of the most literate and able critics of our time. His breadth of reading, acuity of insight, and grace of expression must give most scholars pause; he would no doubt be welcome at any institution in any of the fifty states. But he has remained at a stiff arm's remove from Academe, and has earned his living by the pen alone. In the summer of 1962, however, his resolution wavered and he agreed to teach—at Harvard Summer School. I wanted to remain in Cambridge and therefore applied for the course. It was an offhand decision; I barely had heard of his name. When he accepted me into his fiction workshop, it would have been ungrateful to drop out.

In retrospect I see more clearly how lucky and right was that choice. The first word I wrote for Updike was the first of my first novel. Like any self-respecting undergraduate, I intended to be either a poet, folk-singer, or movie-star. I considered "prose" and "prosaic" to be cognate terms. (They are, admittedly, but I know something more by now about the other three professions and would not trade.) The young man's fancy is poetic, and his models are Rimbaud or Keats. Mine were, at any rate; my first compositions were suicide notes. But I was signed up for a writing workshop with no idea of what to write and not much time to decide. The day of that decision is vivid to me still.

A friend and I were strolling around a lake in Wellesley; we'd been reading for final exams. I heard him out as to his future; then he had to listen to me. I had tried my hand already at the shorter stuff, I said, I was going to write a novel. That was what a summer should consist of—something ambitious, no piddling little enterprise like Chekhov's but something on the scale of, let's say, *Moby Dick*. Yet before I wrote my masterpiece I had to plan it out. What do first novels consist of, I asked—then answered, nodding sagely at a red-haired girl in a bikini emerging from the lake. First novels are either the myth of Narcissus or the parable of the Prodigal Son—but generally disguised. Their authors do not understand they fit an ancient mold. I already knew enough about Narcissus, I confessed, and therefore would elect the latter; I'd rewrite the parable. The difference was that my revision would be conscious—whereas most young novelists fail to see themselves in sufficiently explicit mythic terms.

This was not my problem, but there were problems to solve. I knew nothing about the landscape of the Bible, for instance, and should find a substitute. My friend lit a cigarette; we considered. It happened that I'd been to Greece the previous summer and traveled wide-eyed for weeks. I would replace one location with the other. The parable has three component parts: the son leaves home, spends time away, and returns. My novel too would have three components, with Rhodes and Athens as its locales. My Greek protagonist would go from the island to city and "eat up his substance with whores."

The girl in the bikini trailed drops of water where she

walked; she shook her long hair free. I instructed my friend that hetaerae in Athens had "Follow Me" incised backwards on their sandals, so that they could print directions in the dust. She rounded a bend in the path. The question of contemporaneity engaged me for three minutes. I knew enough about modern-day Greece to fake it, possibly, but knew I'd never know enough about the ways of antique Attica; the prostitute's sandal exhausted my lore. It would take much less research to update the parable. So there, within ten minutes, I had it: a contemporary version of the parable of the Prodigal Son that followed the text faithfully and yet took place in Greece. The rest was an issue of filling in blanks; I started to, next week.

I have told this tongue-in-cheek, but it is nonetheless true. The epigraph of *The Martlet's Tale* is the first line of the parable; the great original is buried in my version, phrase by phrase. I revised the novel many times and by the time I'd finished was no longer a beginner. Looking back I'm astonished, however; it all fell so neatly in place. The editor at Lippincott ushered me into his office and agreed to bring out the book. "You're a very fortunate young man," he said, but I thought his politeness routine. I took success for granted when it came. My photograph in magazines seemed merely an occasion for judging the likeness; a long and flattering review in the *New York Times* on publication day was no more than an author expected; I ate expensive lunches with the cheerful certainty that someone else would pay.

In some degree, moreover, this very blindness worked to my advantage. I had been accustomed to a schoolboy's notion of success. I would have dealt with failure far less equably. Had Updike not encouraged me, I cannot say for certain if I would have persevered; there were many wind-scraps in the wind, and I followed the favoring breeze. Harvard does prepare you for the world in this one crucial way: if you succeed within those walls you assume that you will when outside. When I handed in *The Martlet's Tale*'s first chapter, and my professor's reaction was praise, I concluded that the rest must follow as the night does day. I suppose I stood out in his class; I certainly tried to; his wary approval meant much. I wrote a second chapter and was hooked.

So now we turn from memory to its kissing-cousin, desire. What I would like to tell you, Franz, is how much it meant and means to me to conjure language out of air, to lie for a living and with a straight face. Note also, please—again, our "strange convention of critical discourse"—how "meant" and "means" provide a kind of continuity, how the past shades into present and this repetition-compulsion becomes a kind of oxymoronic refrain. As an imperative the word *refrain* means "stop"; as a component part of rhyme it means, instead, "repeat."

Freud called art "socially validated daydreaming," and the definition, though ungenerous, is apt; I rise early every morning and let out the dog or in the cat and make myself a cup of coffee and sit down to make things up. What I hope for you, my friend, is some version of the pleasure I continue to derive when words edge up against each other in a way that makes them vivid, when the *trompe l'oeil* of engaged imagination makes black marks on a blank page resemble, somehow, reality. Had I instead written "black marks on a white page," for example, the opposition of "black" and "white" would be cognate to but categorically dissimilar from my chosen "black" and "blank." In the first instance the "category" is color, and there's the formulaic juxtaposition of those old wranglers, black and white; in the second it's orthography with perhaps a nod to euphony, the *sound* of black and blank. But how strange to believe that it matters and to sit for twenty minutes while the coffee cools and dawn accretes, attempting to decide . . .

There's a concomitant danger, of course, and you should know that too. "Whom the gods wish to destroy," writes Cyril Connolly, "they first call promising." To stand after four hours of sitting with a paragraph you know to be poor is a strange and particular torture; to feel in your bones that your best is not good enough can harrow the hardiest soul. There is much about this business that simply isn't fun. Almost by definition the young writer models himself on those who succeed; those who fail aren't ours to emulate or read. And your first or fifth book finished merely means you must work at the second or sixth. Though I intend this letter as encouragement and want you, Franz, to stay the course I don't want to delude you as to the charm of our profession or reward of a career; it dwindles more often than not.

"Promise," Connolly concludes, "is that dark spider with which many writers are now wrestling in obscurity and silence."

All this has something to do with the nature of language and our presumed literacy—a natal familiarity with English that, more often than not in the contemporary writer, breeds contempt. No one presumes to give a dance recital without having first mastered the rudiments of dance, to perform Mozart before they've learned scales, or to enter a weight-lifting contest if they've never hoisted weights. Because we've been reading since five, however, we blithely assume we can read; because we scrawled our signature when six, we glibly aspire to write.

Our language is a rich and complex thing, and the conscious, conscientious study of rhetoric has largely disappeared. There are books on the subject, of course, and now and again some Mandarin asseverates that style's a thing to keep. But the keepers of the language-keys are less and less committed to the "high style" as common parlance, or something to aspire to; the various subsets of regional discourse, street-slang and dialect have taken center stage. I don't mean either to praise or deplore this change, mean only to acknowledge it; the time is long since past when we expected our students to master their Latin and muster their Greek. Instead, the injunction, "Know thyself," now seems to suffice for a book . . .

Yet this whole impulse towards self-expression is a recent and possibly aberrant one in art. Legions of accomplished writers found nothing shameful in prescribed or proscribed subjects, nor in eschewing the first-person pronoun. The apprentice in an artist's shop might mix paint for years or learn to dado joints for what must have felt like forever; only slowly and under supervision might he or she approach the artifact as such. Though you come prepared to write your own life's story, or that of a St. Jago's monkey your great-uncle trained while plying the Sargasso Sea, have patience for a season, please; that's not our purpose here.

Nor is "signature" important. The bulk of our literature's triumphs have been collective or anonymous; who can identify the authors of the Bible, the Ramayana or Beowulf? More importantly, who cares? The Illiad and Odyssey are by an unknown bard as are, for all practical purposes, the plays of William Shakespeare. This is not to say that these works don't display personality—the reverse is more nearly true—but rather that the cult of personality should fade. It too is recent and, I think, aberrant; it has nothing to do with the labor of writing as such.

So what I hope you focus on is some particular aspect of our shared craft: a problem you first set and then attempt to solve. The distinction, say, between the simple sentence and complex. Or long and short. A sentence that is one and one that isn't. Or let us further investigate the distinction between a chiasmus and an oxymoron, and if you cannot at this stage distinguish the one from the other you should learn at least a little about the freedom within limits that is the root and force of syntax, that provides, as it were, the art of subjugation, so that we may begin to winnow out what matters from what fails to, what should properly take precedence in the artist's own and chosen hierarchical arrangement—for art *is* hierarchical, a continual adjudication of what counts and what fails to, a way of saying this matters and that doesn't, or at any rate it matters to *me* enough to study and then set it down and my whole course of study will therefore be to make it hereafter and by dint of various manipulations matter to you equally—as others have done to and for me before, as you in your turn will presumably do, because it isn't simple, is it, to return to that bittersweet or enormously small issue of the oxymoron and, enormously bittersweet and small as the distinction might be, chiasmus, or more importantly to argue in this present age and context that such a distinction might matter, that we should give a good goddamn or, provided that this volume can include an even more direct and *pittoresque* alliterative conjunction, a flying fuck—for, although I'll close (not a minute too soon, you seem to be saying, not a sentence or a phrase too few) with the opposite assertion it is no doubt also apposite to asseverate that art is play and cheerfulness keeps breaking through, although admittedly of course and in this narrow compass there are many issues we've not even brought to the table, let alone dissected (note, please, the metaphor implicit in such a trope and soon to be rendered explicit, the comparison of "issues" to a thing-to-be-dissected, a putatively cadaverous—what, cat? skeleton? frog in formaldehyde? fetal pig?—because for me in aging memory it's back and forth again to *Das Ding an sich* if not as yet *thingliness, thingsomeness,* and although there are writers unnumbered who construe their work to be issue-oriented your 'umble servant does not number himself without reservation among them, hoping only and again, again, to make a thing of beauty and to link that non-Euclidean shape with its near-equivalent, truth), so much we've failed to mention about the marketplace, the pleasures of collegiality or horrors attendant on careerism, the contours of a long career as opposed to, by contrast, a short, and there is so much more to say and though good master Pope averred "And ten dull words oft creep in one slow line," I think it's time now to embrace simplicity and stop.

Forgive me, Franz; I've grown as runic and oracular as that fellow who harangued you almost a century since. What it comes down to both at the end and in the beginning is work. In the beginning was the work and work and work. There are many and elegant ways *not* to write, but the definition of a writer is, simply, "one who writes."

And let me also repeat the definition which caused my uncle to declare, "Not bad," the tag-line from Rilke's sustained piece of prose, *The Notebooks of Malte Laurids Brigge.* It seems to me a talisman, a phrase to tack above the writing-desk or underneath the pillow:

"He was a poet. Which is to say, he despised the inexact."
Leben Sie wohl, friend. Take care.

Andre Dubus

Mr. Dubus lists his accomplishments beginning with his declaration that he has six children and five grandchildren. He is the author of nine works of fiction (including his *Selected Stories*) and two collections of essays, most recently *Meditations from a Movable Chair* (1998).

This letter concerns the morality of writing and of the writer, and it is a brave exploration that calls upon us to be brave in turn.

Letter to a Young Writer

I began seriously writing when I was seventeen, a few days after I graduated from high school. By *seriously* I mean that I knew I wanted to write for the rest of my life, and I would need a job to support myself and the family I hoped to have. In the next four years, as a college student, I received three gifts: one from Ernest Hemingway, and two that simply and deeply came to me; from God, I assume; probably He also told me to write a research paper about Hemingway during my freshman year.

I learned from Hemingway to stop each day's work in mid-sentence, while it is still going well, then to exercise the body, and not to think about the story till you go to your desk the next day. Twice, in all these years, I have broken that rule. I was excited, I finished a scene, placed a period at the end of a sentence. The next morning I sat at the desk and could not write. Why? I do not know, but I can guess. A story flows in its own direction, at its own pace, and in it are characters I become while I am writing. They are not me, and my own days and nights take me away from them. I may write on a Wednesday and a Thursday, and between those two times at my desk, I may have to find a plumber, a mechanic, some money; I may exercise, see a movie or a baseball game, talk with people I love, and people I do not, teach, eat, read a story that takes me to nineteenth century Russia where I become a peasant, or to Boston where I become a private detective solving a murder; then there is sleep, with dreams; then waking, a difficulty for some of us (*all life consists of having to get up sooner or later and then having to lie down again sooner or later after a while,* Faulkner wrote in *Old Man*), and caffeine and the newspaper at breakfast, the news frustrating and gloomy, except the baseball stories taking me to spring training in Florida or to last night's or yesterday's game during the season. I think my guess is accurate: it is why, on those two mornings after the mornings when I disobeyed Hemingway's method, I could not enter whatever stories I was writing then, so sat at the desk with a pen, and with paper that remained blank. My soul, for an afternoon and a night, had been spread out and absorbed and it still was, and I did not have the great help of a half sentence, in the middle of a scene, with words—mostly nouns and verbs—written in the margin the day before. Something like this: "She went to the kitchen counter and got a carving knife . . ." Then, in the margin: *sees limes in basket, thinks of margaritas and Baja California with Gretta.*

I write in longhand in notebooks. When I go to my desk I look first at the unfinished sentence and the words in the margin. Then, with a pen in my hand, I turn to the first page of the story and read all that I have written, and I revise, cutting, adding, changing words and punctuation. When I reach the unfinished sentence I do not have to pause; there is at least the remainder of a sentence waiting for me in the margin. Usually more is waiting: there could be a character's memory of being with Gretta in Baja California. This could become a long passage. It could become *the* story, and about Gretta, not about the woman standing at the kitchen counter. She may not even be in the story. *I listen to the voices,* said Faulkner.

The second gift that came to me in college is still a mystery to me. I don't understand how I knew, when I was nearly nineteen years old, that I had to begin sending stories to magazines, knowing that William Faulkner and John O'Hara and Irwin Shaw were also sending stories to magazines, along with God knew who else—writers I had not yet read or even heard of—and knowing that I would not publish a story in *The Saturday Evening Post, Collier's, The New Yorker, Atlantic Monthly, Esquire, Harper's, Mademoiselle,* and so on; yet knowing that I had to submit my work with hope; and knowing that I had to volunteer for rejection, and toughen myself. Volunteering for rejection, so that I could be toughened by it, was the most significant element of that gift, and it remains the most mystifying. Perhaps I began submitting during my nineteenth summer because it was after the spring semester when I had written the paper about Hemingway, and I knew of his years of rejection. I don't know. But I do know that it worked: during the next three years of college, every commercial magazine and the literary quarterlies I knew about rejected my work, and by my senior year this exercise had toughened me. I have never, since then, been deeply hurt or disappointed by the rejection of a story.

In that senior year I received a form letter from *Atlantic Monthly,* asking me to subscribe. I wrote at the bottom of the letter: *When you buy from me, I'll buy from you,* paper clipped it to a story, and mailed it to them. By then, I had willfully forged a false view of editors: if they did not want my work, they were wrong, perhaps crazy; if they wanted my work, they were right, and good. None of this is true, but I still maintain that view; it is armor that protects me from superfluous demons: despair, and vanity, and capitulation of integrity (trying to write for the market, or a particular editor, rather than trying to write a story as it wants to be written). Someone at *Atlantic Monthly,* in 1958, read that note of mine on their form letter, and probably thought I was a cocky fool. I was not cocky. Not about my work; I knew my story was not good enough to be published. I was simply immune to what would happen to a story after I had written it. In 1962, in my fourth year in the Marine Corps—that was the job I had chosen to earn a living—*The Sewanee Review* accepted a story, seven summers after I had begun putting stories where they must be when they are done: in brown manila envelopes addressed to editors. This is a simple thing to say. But I know writers who do not persist. This is a good country for short story writers; we have many fine literary quarterlies, and I believe all good stories will finally be published. Yours will too, if you keep mailing them. I mailed one of mine, "Corporal of Artillery," for seven years. I believe I had to type the first page again because someone had stained it with coffee. *Ploughshares* published it; when I began submitting that story, *Ploughshares* did not exist.

The third gift in college came to me as mysteriously as the first two. Maybe I was thinking about baseball, and this led me to writing; or I was thinking about writing, and this led me to baseball. I knew that pitchers often said that their legs went first, then their arms. So, to postpone natural aging, they had to exercise their legs. This was in the fifties when very few people exercised. I never saw anyone intentionally exercise, except athletes *during* pre-season workouts and the season itself. When I thought of major league pitchers running in the outfield to strengthen their legs, I knew something, suddenly, and it challenged and excited me: my talent as a writer was like a pitcher's arm, a gift I received in my mother's womb. My soul was like a pitcher's legs. I would have to try to be a good human being. I wanted to anyway, but on that day in Louisiana, in that moment in my youth, I knew absolutely that if I did not work to be a good human being, my talent would not last long. The fast ball would slow down, the curve ball would hang, the control would go away.

Somewhere I heard or read that Malcolm Cowley said *No pure son of a bitch ever wrote a good line.* I hope he did say that; he was the sort of man who might have. I will not write confessions here; I will only say that I am still *try*ing to be a good human being, and it is harder work than writing. Sin is part of my life because I am alive. I am not saying that you must be perfect, which is impossible, or free of darkness, also impossible. I am saying that you must want to be a good human being, and make that, too, your vocation. We know that to be a good brother or wife or friend or lover or parent, we must also try to be good people; darkness is antagonistic to love. So why go in darkness to our writing? Emanuel Swedenborg wrote that evil is not human actions but a life of continual ill will. Can you imagine Scrooge, before the ghosts, writing a good story? Any human being, any time, any day, is liable to commit moral felonies or misdemeanors, from anger to gluttony to lust to pride, and so on. But that is neither a whole life nor its direction.

As a writer, you are constantly in training. Day after day, *alone* at your desk, with no one watching you or even depending on you, you take your position on the playing field, try to hit a ninety-five mile an hour fast ball, or throw one. And that is your direction. Part of our vocation, a great part of it, is to love life, therefore human beings. Avoid cynicism. It is an easy flat trail; there are no steep slopes of love to climb; there is no perspiration; human beings, and so love, and so life, are dismissed. I cannot read the work of a cynical writer. Nor can I read the work of a writer who does not have compassion. Why should I? I read to immerse myself into the human heart, through imagined human beings. And in the work of a cynic I will not see the human heart, only the easy flat trail which defends the writer from the hard hills of love and hope and faith. I cannot read the work of a writer who looks down on his characters from the windows of an isolated, proud, condescending room.

Every writer I know is a good human being, which means that each of them wants to be good, and tries to be good. This is not diminished by human weakness and foolishness; I am not writing to you about drunkenness (every writer knows that drinking rusts our tools), making love with the wrong people, fighting and arrogance and pride and vanity, and so on, all those demons that we have to meet in battle. Nor am I writing about happiness or joy or sorrow or dread depression. No, I am telling you that you must work to love, to embrace, to open your soul to the sometimes devastating magnificence of life. I don't think Tolstoy's Ivan Ilych could have written a good story, till his illness. How could he? He did not love. I can read stories written by sad writers, depressed writers, writers driven to the abyss by demons. All art is affirmative, because it shows us that we can survive being mortal. I used to say this to students who were disturbed by stories they felt—and they were right—were depressing. I told them that if a writer has a depressing vision of the world, and can make art out of it, the story is always an affirmation. My friend, the poet Michael Van Walleghen, once said to me that his heroes were Kafka and Kierkegaard, because they lived in the abyss, and kept throwing books out of it.

One more thing: remember chiaroscuro. The photographer Marion Ettlinger explained chiaroscuro to me in 1988. I am grateful to her. Since then, I have tried in each story to see the shadows and the light. Where is the sun? Is it coming through a window? Where is the electric light? Where is the shadow? Does a face reflect the light of a candle? What about the moon and stars and twilight and dusk? When I keep watching the shadows and light I see more of everything physical, and often something metaphysical; sometimes the stories have become about spiritual shadows and light. You will always have shadows, but I hope you will keep moving toward the light.

Pam Durban

Pam Durban is the author of two books of fiction: a collection of short stories, *All Set About with Fever Trees,* and a novel, *The Laughing Place.* Her stories have appeared in many magazines and anthologies, including *New Stories from the South: the Year's Best* (1988 and 1997) and *The Best American Short Stories 1997.* She is the recipient of a Whiting Writer's Award and an NEA Fellowship. She teaches at Georgia State University and serves as fiction editor of *Five Points* magazine.

Ms. Durban diagnoses and addresses a writing pitfall and shows how good writers get over or around it.

That Way He Could Work It

Dear Talented Writer,

Because you *are* that—Thank you for sending me your well-written, stylish story. I was impressed by the care you took with language, the sentence by sentence, moment by moment craft of your piece. Obviously, you are a person of conscience and sensitivity. I must tell you, though, that when I finished the last paragraph of your story, where the man looks at the dying deer he's just hit with his car and thinks it must be an omen of something but can't figure out of *what,* I turned the page, looking for the real ending and, not finding it, sat down to write you this letter.

In one of *his* letters, Chekhov wrote that the writers we call "eternal or simply, good, the writers who intoxicate us, have one highly important trait in common: they are moving towards something definite and beckon you to follow, and you feel with your entire being, not only with your mind, that they have a certain goal, like the ghost of Hamlet's father, which had a motive for coming and stirring his imagination." And yet, if the ghost of Hamlet's father were to appear in your story or dozens, *hundreds* like it that flow through magazine offices and graduate workshops, the story might treat him like this: "Hamlet lit a cigarette and walked to the edge of the parapet. How long had it been since he'd slept? He couldn't remember. A long time. As he stood there, the ache around his heart returned. Then the ghost of his father appeared before him. 'Son,' the ghost said, 'my brother murdered me and now he's sleeping with your mother, my wife.' His father vanished. Hamlet walked to the edge of the parapet and stared out into the night. His father's ghost. It must mean something, he thought, but what? what? as, alone, he wept in the darkness." The End. Notice how flimsy it all is, a tissue of vague emotion made of darkness and tears. Weeping, by the way, is another way in which too many stories refuse to engage their own possibilities. Floods of tears blur the feeling in these stories, as do receding tail lights in the rain and other images of generic emotion, usually a variety of sadness. What you've written here is probably *the* contemporary formula story: it begins with a wounded self and ends with a vague image of uncomprehending vulnerability without once *grappling* with the *subject* of vulnerability or passivity or cruelty or blindness.

It wasn't so much that your *character* didn't understand what he'd lived through in the story. Fiction is full of characters who lack insight into their lives and situations. Bartleby, the Scrivener, in Melville's story, or Little Chandler in Joyce's "A Little Cloud," or Royal Earle Thompson in Katherine Anne Porter's "Noon Wine," or just about any character in an early Raymond Carver story. Nor is it necessary for the end of a story to dazzle the reader with insight or for a story to shut with an audible click. Chekhov called what he was trying to do at the end of a story shifting the center of gravity in order to provoke maximum thought. The endings of many of his stories open quietly into further complexity. An Alice Munro story often ends by questioning its own conclusions. But in none of these cases does the *story* refuse to engage its subject; nor do any of the stories I've mentioned deny by offering blank, stunned numbness as the conclusion of their characters' journeys, that *something* significant has just happened.

The trouble with these contemporary formula stories and the ends they come to is that by refusing to engage their own possibilities they destroy themselves. If the ending of a story is vague and pointless, then none of the actions that led to the vague and meaningless conclusion can be seen to have caused or brought about anything, and the whole story collapses. Over and over again, these stories that offer a reader a wash of generalized emotion end with the literary equivalent of *whatever,* the shrug with which one turns away from trouble.

Good fiction, the kind of fiction you want to write and I want to write, is sturdier than that; it is sharper and more unflinching. It does not turn away. Good writers cultivate the habit of, to use Toni Morrison's word, *unblinkingness.* Good writers write stories that don't simply *reflect* something, they *frame* a character or situation so that we see not simply a portrait of a shivering and frightened victim of some unnameable wrong, or a gesture in the general direction of sadness, but something particular about *this* fear, *this* passivity, *this* sadness. At their best, stories give us a way to see *into,* to infer consequences, to perceive a pattern in what has just been lived through. At their best, stories trace in heightened and specific detail the entanglements of character and situation and contribute valuable new words with which to name the varieties of human response.

How do they do that? And what do writers see when they stare unblinkingly at a character? I think they see, not a general outline or a shadow, but Chekhov's *something definite.* They see particular individuals living their particular moments and reaching particular outcomes. That is what you notice in interesting and engaging narratives: their clarifying particularity. I think of the ending of Katherine Anne Porter's "Noon Wine," the moment just before the suicide of Royal Earle Thompson. In that story's last paragraph, Mr. Thompson, doomed by his inability to shoulder the moral weight of his murder of another man, removes his right boot and sock, lies on the ground with the mouth of the shotgun pressed under his chin and feels for the trigger with his great toe. And yet, terrible as these actions are, it is not simply his imminent suicide that we are being asked to contemplate; it is the devastating truth of the story's last sentence: "That way he could work it." This powerful sentence focuses our attention on the moment when this man whose life has ceased to work (and we know the particulars of that failure now because the rest of the story has given them to us) discovers how to work the shotgun trigger with his toe. The word *work* echoes through the rest of the story like the shotgun blast that follows it but which we do not hear. What we are left with is a horrifying, precise image of this particular response to the particular failures of Mr. Royal Earle Thompson's life.

So here's the useful part, the hopeful part. What you have to do to give your stories weight and depth is to think hard and long, carefully and clearly and with compassion about your characters as individuals whose lives and situations are unique. To develop in yourself what Robert Coles calls a "moral imagination" which may be, it occurs to me, the same thing as Morrison's unblinkingness—the capacity to see how meaning and consequence develop in an individual's life as a result of his or her actions and then to give us that uniqueness in the particulars you choose to build your fictional world. Particulars are essential because they are the means by which a writer brings a reader into intimate contact with his story. And once we readers are brought close that way, made intimate, we cannot be indifferent onlookers, and that's the point. Kafka's "axe for the frozen sea inside," that definition of a good story's effect, is sharpened on the particulars of character and situation.

So, your job is to grab us and bring us close and say "Look, this is what happened. This person made these choices, she made these mistakes and these lucky swerves and look where it got her." What you have to do is to show us how the abyss you're nudging your character toward the brink of is a unique geographical feature of a particular landscape, and when you push him or her over the edge, to let us hear that the sound of the voice of someone falling into that abyss registers terror in an individual key.

Sincerely,
Pam Durban

Shelby Foote

A writer of excellent fiction—*Tournament, Follow Me Down, Love in a Dry Season, Shiloh*—Shelby Foote is also the author of great history in the form of his massive and brilliant three volumes on the Civil War. Foote and Percy, who wrote six novels ranging from very good to great, were friends since their teenage years in Greenville, Mississippi.

Here, Foote teaches and preaches with charm and passion about the nature of fiction.

Letter to Walker Percy

Monday: 18 Feb 52

Yesterday's letter as I remember it was far too snappish and dogmatic. Let me elaborate a bit. As for perversity and uncharitableness, I think you ought to understand that my attitude toward what I was condemning is at least comparable to what Christ Himself felt toward the moneychangers. And let me elaborate on that; here is my point: I think a writer's mistakes are infinitely more interesting than any editor's "corrections" (and mind you, a critic is only an editor-once-removed)—I think no one can have the view of the book the writer himself has, the CREATIVE view, the containing of the force that brought it into being. It sometimes happens that certain scenes have no evident function; the critic says, Take this out. But these very scenes work in some way to bring out the total effect, heighten the contiguous scenes, and give the whole book its peculiar individuality. Yet any smart editor would have cut them—I'm not talking about a dummy, I mean really *smart:* the speed of the book would be picked up, the reading would go better, it would have "drive." But dont you see? it wouldnt be the same book; above all, it wouldnt be the writer's book. And God knows what effect this would have on that same writer's following work. A man must learn from his mistakes (even granting he was wrong)—from MAKING them, not from being saved from them.

I'll go still further. A good writer *never* makes a mistake in a basic sense: not when he is writing of things that matter to him—and when he is not doing that, no amount of editing can correct it; the fault will be so intrinsic that *no* amount of editing can correct it. All the editor can do is make it "readable" (for Godsake!) or artistically "interesting" (for Godsake!). . . . Dont you see?

I am talking about something that I think is the most important thing in the world. I think really you must not take this wrong tack at the start. For God's sake, Walker, do not listen to anyone who would try in any way to tell you how to shape a book; above all, dont listen to anyone who would tell you how to REshape a book. . . . Now I may be wrong: maybe they didnt tell you any such thing; maybe they just wrote in general terms about what you should do about preparing for your future writing of *other* books. Thats all right, especially as for recommending reading you should do—but the other is pure poison, of a kind that is unremovable, malignant.

(Here I wound up even more snappish & dogmatic.)

I think each book has its own problems. All a writer can do is tackle it on its own terms, see it the clearest he can, and then sail in. Each is a voyage beset by shoals. If he fails, he fails and thats most miserable . . . but there is a great resource left—there will be other books and other problems; life is long and the individual facets of Art are fleeting, except of course in the long view: which no writer ever takes, being a peculiar sort of fool, & therefore wise.

Part of this difference between us proceeds from a basic difference of approach. You, I think, believe that you have something to TELL people, and youd appreciate any help from anywhere that you thought would enable you to TELL them this thing more effectively; also you have a sort of modesty. I'm different on both counts. I dont want to TELL anybody anything; I want to SHOW them—I believe that is the only way to tell them; I want to communicate a view of the world; I think thats true wisdom. So that our difference springs from the fact that you think my end-endeavor is merely a stop on the way and you are willing to jump over it, take the word of others as to how to accomplish it—you want to get by it as swiftly and effectively as possible. . . . Youre so wrong. Youll come before long to see that I am right; wisdom is frequently just an ability to see that you passed the really important point somewhere back down the line—as in this case. DONT PASS IT; STOP AND SEE WHAT I'M TRYING TO EXPLAIN. If you let anyone fiddle with your way of seeing—fiddle deliberately, I mean: not by example but by pointing out—youll nick this instrument beyond repair; youll wind up with nothing but regrets.

Let me illustrate. Take any really great piece of work; take the Ode to a Nightingale. What is he telling?—namely, that this bird sang in longgone times and all men are connected by such sensations; that youth is difficult because it is all feeling and no wisdom. It's a good thought, certainly. But what did he TELL you?—only that, and not nearly so clearly as I state it. . . . But now go back and read the Ode. Wherein lies its greatness? Certainly not in what the poem TELLS you. Dont you see? . . . Now imagine Keats getting help from Leigh Hunt (or whoever—and mind you, Leigh Hunt was quite a fellow in his day, though now we know better)—imagine Hunt reading the first draft and saying, "You dont have quite the pitch in this stanza. 'Deceiving elf'—thats a villainous pair of words; you need something stronger at this point," and so forth. . . . And dont think, because youre not the writer Keats was, that you can accept lower standards; you cant; you are obliged to think your every page is another Nightingale—thats one of the gambits of the game; and if you play by other rules, youre not a writer, youre a journalist or (for Godsake!) a teller of parables for imbeciles. . . . Also dont object on grounds that Keats was writing POETRY. The rules are no different, not now that the novel has come of age; it's a dedicated calling. You criticised me once for writing for "angels"—and so I do. The dirty minds, the slow wits, the critics with their pick-brain tendencies: these people must be ignored in the creative process. Nothing but ruin can come of even considering them. A man must write for himself, and then he must accept the penalties—including the possibility of damnation. Youve got to put it all on the line; anything less than *all* is hedging and your work is weakened at the wellspring, hopelessly flawed, shot through with rot. Not to mention the sapping of vitality; thats what hurts.

Now take SHILOH, which you say you like. It doesnt TELL anybody a damned thing. Can you for one minute think I should have let anyone on the big green earth step between me and the paper to guide my pen? . . . Or the others, for that matter. FOLLOW ME DOWN, which you dont like (and youre so wrong): Do you think I should listen to your talk about being ashamed I wrote it? Certainly not, for the fact is it contains a whole new world of good and evil, seething with them, and it was a step along the way in developing a style. TOURNAMENT, too—which contains errors in judgment on every page, errors the damndest fool critic on earth could correct: Do you think I, as a writer, would have benefitted from having these corrections made before the book went into print? Certainly not. DRY SEASON, which is little more than an exercise in the manipulation of plot (or plots) covered by a certain brilliance of style, is a book they say I shouldnt have done at all. Balls! . . . Dont you see? The only thing is to pay no attention to anyone at all.

Except me, of course. But I'm wise; I dont hand out specific advice; I just rare back and beller, and that cant do any harm beyond tickling your risibilities perhaps.

Believe me:
Shelby

John Gardner

John Gardner (1938–1982) was known as much for his ability to get at the inner workings of the fiction of others, and for his ability to instruct, as for his superb novels and stories, which include *Grendel, The Sunlight Dialogues, The King's Indian,* and *October Light.* His *The Art of Fiction* and *On Becoming a Novelist* are permanently useful.

In this very specific letter to the novelist Joanna Higgins, Gardner demonstrates the size of his heart as well as the depth of his knowledge.

Letter to Joanna Higgins

Dear Joanna,

HILL OF LIGHT—very few comments. I'd start in 3rd omniscient, avoid the immediate leap into third limited, go to third limited with the words (p. 2) *But this!* Matter of taste. Avoiding 3rd limited at first makes the opening less pushy, lets you earn the emotion outright, not seem overeager to suck the reader in.

. . .

FIRE NOTEBOOK. But the tense business is minor, a fairly easy matter for rethinking and rewriting. The piece has more important problems, the chief of which is this: it doesn't deliver. You set things up then seem to abandon them, or maybe get confused. What happens to the Bishop? We're following him, very interested, and then suddenly we're hearing about a parson, then later about a pastor (who seems to be intended as the same person—but the two languages are different, suggesting different sects). Is the parson a different person or the same one as the pastor, the Bishop? I know I could sit and figure this out, but I don't think I should have to; you're the one telling the story.

I think you have a really great story by the left hind leg, but so far you haven't really got it captured. So far it doesn't have real *design* and it only plays around at having *meaning*. If the parson is different from the Bishop, the parson should be introduced earlier and the Bishop (dead or otherwise) should reappear. (I *guess* the Bishop doesn't die. I *guess* the church is spared or something, and the parson is the Bishop—though Bishops aren't parsons. But I don't really care about working such things out, I leave them to you.) What I mean by *design*

157

is design in its most literal sense—this balances that, this explains that, and so on. The story ends with an essayish focus on language (a good section); I think that focus should show up earlier and should be subtly, brilliantly explored in the story. (You have some of this: comforting texts, etc—and one spot I don't believe, the Devil spouting Milton.) Design would suggest that perhaps (not certainly) the "man" at the end (reading newspapers, etc) should show up near the beginning—or something. Design suggests that anything emotionally important in the story—Prybilski at his millwork, the schoolteacher and kids, etc—should appear not only in the short scenes they're given but should in one way or another suffuse the story, either literally or symbolically. . . .

Which takes me to my second point, meaning. What makes the story unsatisfying in its present form is that the meaning hasn't really been hunted down, what you come up with is too easy. For a brief period in the history of literature, the good got rewarded and the bad got punished (roughly 17th through 19th centuries). That no longer seems entirely adequate. 20th century fiction at its most Christian and optimistic (or generally religious and optimistic) says, as earlier stories of yours do . . . that the reward is subtle and inward. That's still tenable, I think. There really is something blessed about the good—my father and mother when their life is knocked out from under them by my father's stroke are strangely happy, however battered; or consider that sixth man on the tail of the plane last week in Washington. You've believed this and have written brilliant fiction on the basis of that belief, but in THE FIRE NOTEBOOK you are clearly tempting devils and—I think—ducking back from their fire. In this story, the Devil is terrible, mighty, and indifferent, amused. That his power is very great is evident; but what that power is your story seems a little uncertain about. . . . I can't really intuit a metaphysic or, more loosely, theory. What I suspect, perhaps wrongly, is an easy-out optimism. What am I supposed to make of the miracle of the bells? (I don't ask for a scientific explanation, though you may know one—in fact I'd be disappointed to hear one, though I of course suspect some such explanation can be found.) What I ask is only that, here as elsewhere, the story *deliver.* You set up the miracle, you interested me, you can't just leave me high and dry. Does the woman die, despite the miracle and her vision before it? [It doesn't matter either way, I just need to know so I can figure it into the equation.] When the Bishop is set down right where he started, after his trip with the Devil, is he a better man *because* of the Devil's work? In spite of it? Or what? Does he live or die? [does it matter?]. The 19th-century style poet we encounter at the end I'd like to have encountered earlier; but either way, what am I to think? One reader could say, "This is bad poetry: Tragedy in real life mostly leads to crap poetry"; another: "This is bad poetry, but good-hearted, trapped in its time and imitativeness but deeply serious, therefore full of God." Is one answer right, the other wrong? Are both right? You don't really have to tell me in the story, but I have to feel you've decided, more or less, in your own mind.

Bill Spanos has made me leery of fiction that's too neat, too dogmatic; but I think it's infinitely important that, whether or not it comes up with answers, fiction should think. My guess is that, up to this draft, you've been controlled by your material, have not yet risen above it to where you can use it for real and deep meditation. THE HILL OF LIGHT is in my opinion a philosophically profound work, as well as dramatically powerful. THE FIRE NOTEBOOK in my

opinion is still undigested, mainly, I think, because it chal
lenges your Christian optimism: you haven't yet faced the
Melvillian or Twainian risk. I think that by your character you
can never finally be a nihilist. What the devout Taoist says, "If
a fool were to learn the Truth he would laugh aloud," I would
say of you—also of me. The truth is, to me, grotesquely simple: God is Love, and Love's weakest extension is matter, and
we are both matter and God, but most noticeably matter. (I
think that's in HILL OF LIGHT, in different words.) But the
very fact that you're protected in advance (by your character,
by which I mean your early religious optimism, which is now
in the blood) makes it vital that you face the questions truthfully and fully, because those who try to face them with no
psychological ground to stand on can be helped (in the medical sense "saved") by you.

What are you talking about in FIRE NOTEBOOK? Free Will
and Determinism; Love and Will; Spirit and Matter; Pride and
Humility; Fate and Chance; Justice and Injustice; Events and
Words. What is the dramatic focus? Catastrophe and
Response. What is it that emotionally involves you as a writer
and as a person in the story told here? 1) Unthinkable as it
was, it really happened, and to people related to you. (It's
important, I think, to remember that this is the chief power
of the piece for you. One does not choose one's subjects for
aesthetic or philosophical reasons. And knowing one has chosen this story for the reason I've given, one can justly indulge
oneself in detail: your fascination will communicate itself and
make the story crackle.) 2) It seems a story of monstrous
injustice and horror. If you make it anything else than that
you will be lying about your emotion and the historical fact.
Your present version does not come off as horrible or tragic.

The Devil, as a non-realistic creature, slightly distances the story: he is not a metaphor for the sickness at heart you feel as you read old clippings (as he should be) but an artifice by means of which you can hold the pain at arm's length. In my opinion, the thing that first attracted you to the story, the flat-out horror and injustice, is distanced and muted by every device you choose—which is not to say you should use different devices, but only to say that you must master the devices, not be enslaved by them. Your characters tend toward stereotype. . . . You give brilliantly vivid descriptions of how things catch fire, but you shrink from real human psychology—the second by second responses of the people caught. The result is a curious frigidity that I think most readers wouldn't catch, something like the decadence one sees in comic books, where every surface is brilliantly rendered but all the characters are familiar. In short, to tell this story and completely de-fuse your original reason for telling it is to ruin the story. (Look again at *Under the Volcano*.) There are two wrong ways of telling the story: a) nihilistically, as a proof that life is shit; b) optimistically, as a proof that Though April showers, may come your way, they bring the Flowers, that bloom in May. 3) It affords you a chance to do an authentically modern (contemporary) piece of fiction. This work is like nothing you've ever done before—"experimental." I hope you won't underestimate that impulse. Here's how it goes, in my opinion. A writer wants only one thing: to thrill his reader, not for egoistic purposes (on the writer's part) but because the writer is thrilled by good writing and wants to give to others (readers) what he/she has received (from great writers). Part of what pleases us in new fiction is its novelty. A splendid new way of telling a story is valuable in itself—otherwise there would be no Lardner, Hemingway, Faulkner, Barthelme, and so on. . . .

As Melville said once (unless I made it up, a thing I'm prone to) "Mine deeper, that's the ticket!" (Surely I made it up.) Expand, develop, think harder, make a design!

. . .

Yours,
John

George Garrett

Born in Florida in 1929, Mr. Garrett is author of thirty books (most recently *Days of Our Lives Lie in Fragments,* 1998) and is editor or coeditor of seventeen others. He is Henry Hoyns Professor of Creative Writing at the University of Virginia.

One of the most accomplished teachers of writing here gives something of a lesson about—among other elements in the writer's life—anger.

You Are Adam and You Are Eve

The principal business of the writer is always in the details, with specific things. Generalizations and abstraction are the enemies of our art and the process of creating it. And this applies to our critical as well as our creative actions. We always need to be talking about specific stories or texts and in detail.

Nevertheless, I am going to break my own rule—and always remember that rules, though they have to be known and understood, challenge you to break them—and say some very general things about our craft and art. What I am going to talk about applies (and here's another big fat generalization to deal with) to all forms of writing, really. The same general rules apply to poetry, the essay, forms of nonfiction, drama, indeed all the familiar forms of narrative. Insofar as there is a story involved, even the lyric story, the mouthful of air of a lyric poem, the same general rules apply. The modern divorce, separation, and segregation of one kind of writing, one form and another, from the others, this kind of special-ization is really very new in the long history of literary tradi-tion. From well before Homer until after John Dryden, this was understood. One form, the epic, the pastoral, the romance, what-have-you, might hold a place of honor in the hierarchy of value. And that constantly changed with the changing times. All forms, whether in verse or prose, were part of the same continuum, chips off the same essential block, different, like sins, in degree not kind; therefore differ-ent from each other only in superficial ways.

Why should you care that, like lovers in the dark, all liter-ary forms are essentially the same? For a couple of reasons. One is that, once you understand this general truth, you can learn equally well from examining any of them. You will find that you can be, indeed already are influenced by other literary forms—poems, essays, the movies, and (alas) television, you name it. Secondly, and this is a more complex generalization: if all forms are at heart the same, as I'm claiming here, different only in degree not kind, then you as a writer, a maker of anything and any form, are not only related to other writers, however dimly, in kind, but you are in fact up to exactly the same thing as any and all of them—Homer, Shakespeare, Tolstoy, Virginia Woolf, all of them. Even at their most wonderful and triumphant moments they are only different from you in degree. This is a serious thought. A source of pride. But also a source of enormous humility. To share this art you owe them all, the great ghosts and the living, nothing less than the best you can possibly muster. Whether you succeed or fail is mostly irrelevant, since in large part success or failure (however they are measured and defined) are out of your hands and mine. But you do have the choice to withhold nothing, to give nothing less than not only your best effort, but all you've got. That giving can be measured; "good" and "bad" cannot be measured. As to the relativity of good and bad, I offer you the statement of the novelist and poet Joyce Cary about this in terms of Gulley Jimson, the painter and protagonist of *The Horse's Mouth*. Of Jimson, Joyce Cary writes that it does not matter whether he was rated as a good artist or a bad one, but that he was and is an artist, a creator. Cary writes: "He is himself a creator, and has lived in creation all his life, and so he understands and continually reminds himself that in a world of everlasting creation there is no justice. The original artist who counts on understanding and reward is a fool."

Another general word or two about the past, the literary

past. First, it is all simultaneous. That is, for a writer the literary past, our tradition and our history, is neither strictly chronological nor evolutionary. Forms change and fashions change, habits develop and are played out; but for us, as writers, Homer and Shakespeare and Hemingway are simultaneously past and can be equally influential. And they all have things to teach us. Secondly, there is the problem that none of us knows enough about our own literary past or indeed, our own literary present. None of us, not you and not I, reads as much as we ought to, knows as much as we have to. This is not a weight of knowledge that should be allowed to stifle or silence us. Not by any means. It should be allowed to liberate us. Unless we labor to know and to understand as much as we possibly can of our literary history and tradition, we are condemned each generation to re-invent the wheel or the sail with great surprise and fanfare.

As to the present, in one sense that is even more important. Because, like it or not, know it or not, we are coming along in time at the tag end of our century and its traditions. That can't be helped. The times are changing all the time. We owe it to ourselves to understand and to appreciate the best that our contemporaries have achieved. Judging by myself and my students, past and present, I safely conclude that we are too ignorant for our own good.

Generalizations: unless you love to read and read as much as you are able to, frivolously as well as wisely and well, you will not be much of a writer.

Things will change. They always do. But it is the burden of all of us, coming to our art and craft in the last years of this century, that we have to be self-conscious, to know what we are doing. I do not mean to encourage this kind of self-consciousness in the actual act of creation, the creative process, the first searching vision and draft of what we do. We all go at this differently, and the only good advice I can give you is what I have always told my students. Trust your original impulse. Trust the muse completely until she proves to be, beyond the shadow of a doubt, unfaithful. But after vision comes revision. That's another thing, a bag of tricks and then some. You need to know, confidently, that during revision you can fix anything, change anything to suit yourself. Revision is what we really talk about in our classes and workshops. The creative process is a little like taking a bath. Other people can help you do it, but they can't do it for you. Another simile: you shape and sculpt clay to form, but it comes to life, with the breath of your life, in revision. All of us would rather not have to revise anything at all. Just put it through the typewriter or into the computer, perfect and complete the first time, effortlessly. Pure inspiration. No sweat and strain and doubt. And that happens, probably will happen once or twice in your lifetime. And that will always seem to be the best time, the way it ought to be. But through the labor, sometimes hard labor, you will discover what every good writer does, that you can make a work seem to be the effortless result of pure inspiration.

Another brief digression. A general word about what we do. We try always to tell the truth. But we deal in the ways and means of seems. A good story is not inevitable, first sentence to last. Never is. *It only seems to be inevitable.* That seeming comes from authority. You are the author. Use your authority to make your story, your poem, your play seem to be absolutely inevitable even though you and I know it is a string of choices and compromises powered by an original impulse. Be true to that impulse, but also be sly, cunning, crafty in revision. Over the years I have come to know many other writers, even some successful ones. Many are not very intelligent. Some are not even very talented. But I defy you to tell which are which. Thanks to the power of revision they are the equals of anybody alive.

Now we need, at least, to be introduced to a few more problems or questions, some more particular generalizations about the natural magic of our art and about how to deal with our adversary in this business. Our adversary is not the reader. The reader is an ally and shares in the experience evoked by our work. Our adversary is the editor, the publisher. They stand between you and your reader, and you need to understand in general what they are up to and how to deal with them. There are too many practical details to deal with here. But there are some general things, attitudes, to be explored now.

First then, a couple of notions about our art. These are things I came to slowly, the hard way. Therefore I am eager to proclaim and share them, obvious as they may be.

The fuel of all narrative, what the machine runs on, is suspense. The image isn't idle, because all narrative, interior as well as exterior, eventful or not, calls for forward motion. Coaches always used to tell runners not to look back. You lose more than a step every time you break your running rhythm to sneak a peek over your shoulder. A narrative is a run for it without serious interruption. The suspense is not merely a matter of what happens next. It also includes the questions *who are these guys* and *what's going on here*. And it is not at all a conflict between the ways of showing and telling. Of course, we want to dramatize as much as possible, to show and let the reader, deeply engaged in the flow of experience of the narrative, infer and discover things. But we have to find ways to tell, also. Show what you can and have to and tell what you must, but do so with suspense. Keep the reader moving to keep up with you. Don't tell any more than you have to and don't tell until you have to. Information and exposition are the areas of craft where the amateurs, even the gifted ones, stumble and reveal themselves.

One little general rule worth remembering is that the more the narrative, by plot and nature, has a built-in suspense, the less you have to impose suspense upon it. And (more important) vice versa. If your story doesn't have a whole lot of suspense, do it the way comics do a shaggy dog story. Divert attention with details.

By the way, the same basic rule applies to funny and sad, comedy and tragedy. If your story is inherently comic, you don't need funny one-liners and the like. If it's sad, let the reader arrive at that conclusion; don't twist the reader's arm.

What all this adds up to is the necessity, at some point, vision or revision, of knowing the essential nature of the material in your story line. It is urgently important that you know the feelings your narrative summons up from a receptive reader.

If suspense is the gasoline that narrative runs on, repetition and redundancy are the chief causes of breakdown. Don't repeat yourself if you can help it. Make a point, only one time if possible, and then move on to the next one. If during revision, you find that you have made the same point more than once, what that usually means is that you haven't made up your mind precisely where that point should be made.

Writing is an art, like and unlike any other art. What defines any art is that it is, first and foremost, a sensuous affective experience. What this means is that the first thing that happens between you and the reader, the original seduction, is that you must evoke and engage the senses. That is more important than plot, action, character, structure. First you must convince your reader that your narrative, whether it pretends to be "real" or professes to be pure fantasy, is sensibly perceptive. Use all five senses early and as often as possible. Somehow this becomes the magic spell that makes everything else work.

A third hobby horse I like to ride on: once you understand what is going on in your narrative and what it seems to be about, in revision go against the grain of it as often as possible. Your bad guys will be bad; so deliberately let them have some good traits. Give the good guys more bad habits. This will give characters more dimension and complexity.

Your greatest single choice is, once you understand your own work, whether to go with the grain, to follow the expectations the subject raises or to take the direction John Keats advocated and surprise us "with a fine excess." Surprise is almost as important as suspense.

What all this adds up to is the fact that your chief enemy, as an artist, is the stereotype, any stereotype. To create something new and worthwhile, question all stereotypes, good and bad, and all the assumptions behind them, good and bad. You are Adam and you are Eve, every day at your desk. Name the things of this world. Do not doubt your initial impulse. Faced with rejection and indifference, you are bound to doubt your talent sometimes. Fight against that doubt and try to believe in your talent, be it ever so humble. But turn all the full force of your doubts and skepticism against the common assumptions of your age and especially against all of your own certainties.

Of course, successful dealing with magazine editors and with publishers asks for something else. They are in the rejection business. If you are in the fiction editorial office of, say, the *Atlantic Monthly,* you receive about 12,000 stories a year in the mail and you will publish maybe 12 of them. Think— no, imagine how that would be. The writer must be able to imagine the self wearing somebody else's shoes. I find many writers, even good and experienced ones, unable or unwilling to imagine what an editor really does for a living, how editors judge and evaluate the manuscripts that come to them. No one who judges 12,000 manuscripts in search of 12 can be taken completely seriously as a fair judge or an arbiter of taste.

Consider what this means. Yes, that quality, except for some things instantly recognizable, that is literary stereotypes, does not and cannot possibly enter much into the process beyond the most rudimentary reactions. By any logical standard, from your point of view, there is no sense, no rhyme or reason to any of it. From your point of view it's a crapshoot. Try to bear in mind the editor's point of view. From that angle it's all part of something quite outside of your ken and control—putting together the best possible issue of the magazine. In that process and to that end, you and your life's work are as expendable as the infantry in World War I.

This knowledge need not be depressing. One thing that it means is that you would be wasting your time to follow the example of the earlier generations of American writers in this century and try to write for some particular market or magazine. What you are left with is at once more simple and more demanding. It does not make any sense at all to write to or for anybody's standards but your own. It is as difficult to write bad fiction as it is to write well. Since there is no point in it, anyway, why waste your time and talent on anything else but what moves you, what you believe in? It is your best chance, your only chance.

There are all kinds of ways to shorten the odds against you. But there is no escaping the truth that not editors or publishers or agents or anybody else but yourself is able to judge your effort. Nobody else can help or harm you much.

To endure and maybe even prevail you need to train and test yourself against the pain of rejection. You need to be tough as old shoe leather without losing your sensitivity. So I am going to end this letter, appropriately, with a story. That's what we are all about, isn't it, stories, not rules to be observed or broken?

Recently I was asked to write a piece about my experience (not yet over and done with by a long shot) of rejection. It has been a painful experience remembering and resurrecting moments from a lifetime of rejections. Here is just one of them, but one which says it as well as I can, one of the rejections of my novel, *Death of the Fox,* devastating at the time. In the end there was a happy ending for that book. But at the time the future of that book and its author looked bleak.

I begin in the middle of the story.

And so began some eighteen months, with and without benefit of agent, of submitting the manuscript of *Death of the Fox* to a long string of publishers. Who rejected it. More than a dozen. All the time I continued to polish and revise the manuscript according to my own lights; for nobody had any suggestions. They would hold it awhile, sometimes months, then simply reject it.

For the first time with any of my books I began to be seriously, deeply worried that it would never find a publisher. My anxiety was acute after Robert Gottlieb of Alfred Knopf rejected it. He had especially asked to see it from my agent, Perry Knowlton. Knowlton seemed excited by Gottlieb's interest, because, he explained to me, Gottlieb was something of an expert on both Ralegh and Elizabethan times and was very eager to publish something in that area. It was submitted to him and several months passed. I was later to learn that during a part of that time Mr. Gottlieb had been on jury duty and was, of course, unable to deal with my manuscript.

I remember that I was at a remote ranch in Wyoming with my family, the nearest phone many miles away, when I got a message to call Knowlton at once. I came down to the little crossroads called Moose and placed my call, figuring it had to be good news. For bad news, just another rejection, he could more easily have written. I was (almost; I am wary) elated. I had (still do) an enormous respect for Knopf and for the celebrated Mr. Gottlieb. Wouldn't that be something, huh? I told myself as I drove down the long, twisty, dusty little dirt road towards Moose. There is a place along that road where you sometimes see some elk browsing. And there they were. I took that for a very good sign.

Over the crackle and static of the phone I gathered from Knowlton that Gottlieb had turned it down. It seemed, as he explained it to me, that the subject and structure were all right, but the language (the *words,* you see) was inadequate and it just didn't work at all.

Well.

Not much I could do about that, was there? Not even if I wanted to. I could maybe begin again on page one and change all the words. . . .

I drove back the long climbing drive, with its wild and spectacular views of the mountains, first in a dust-rolling fury, then more slowly. Trying my best to create a mask and a manner to be able to break the news gently, with at least a little swagger and bravado.

I think of all the rejections I have experienced that was the one that (suddenly and for no sound reason) wounded me most. A knife in the guts. I have to confess to a great folly, all the more foolish coming from someone as experienced as I was. I would guess now that not one day has gone by, certainly no working day, in which the memory of that pain and the shame of that moment has not flashed in my mind. In which a massive fury has not risen up from my bowels to my lips at the thought and memory, a fury mercifully able to be checked by my mind, functioning reasonably, and by my less rational faith and upbringing. Which faith turns the blame on myself for allowing myself the luxury and vice of hating another human being (in this case someone utterly unknown to me, no more than a name) with an unforgiving and murderous malice.

After that reaction I hear the inner laughter and deceptively soft voice of my secular doorman, Mr. Worldly Wise, ridiculing me. "Either find a way to get even, study revenge, or forget it."

I hold my inner ears and try to go on working.

I remember a story about a good and true friend. During World War II in Basic Training he developed a case of blisters and continued marching on them until his feet were terribly infected. Went to Sick Call. Where a Medic, who had not yet even examined his feet, ridiculed him and accused him of malingering. Then the Medic yanked off one bloody sock, peeling off the whole raw sole of the foot and causing a great pain to my friend. But, more serious and annoying to the Medic's point of view, causing blood to flow free in gouts all over the Medic's recently mopped and clean floor. It was most likely the mess that startled and upset the Medic most.

My friend was put, briefly, in the hospital to heal up. Never saw the Medic again. True, they were in the same division, but a division is a very large military unit, many thousands of men.

Then one day, three years later, in the closing days of the War, most of my friend's platoon, and all of his best friends, were killed in one brisk and savage fight against an SS unit. When it was over my friend suddenly knew what he had to do to make up for his terrible loss. He found a truck going to the rear and hitched a ride back some miles to the chief division medical center. He was fully armed; his M-1 loaded, with a full clip and one round chambered, and locked. From out of the buried past the Medic's name had emerged as shiny and bright as if written in neon. And it was my friend's firm intention to find that man, if he could be found, and to kill him, thus evening the score. He hated that man far more than he hated any of the SS troopers he had been fighting. True, they had been trying to kill him, but there was nothing personal about it.

The end of the story is this. My friend located and hunted down his victim. Arrived at an aid station just at dark in a light rain. Bloody busy work by Coleman lantern light, groans and cries of the wounded, urgency everywhere. It was there that he found out his enemy had been killed that same afternoon by an artillery shell which had landed in the general area of the aid station. Killed instantly, they said.

My friend stood there in the mud in a rainswept darkening field and, laughing like a movie lunatic, fired all nine rounds in his M-1 into the sky.

Then he was all right again. Ready to go back to the War. To kill or be killed.

I understand that story deeply. Sometimes when I am swept with a rush of shame and anger too strong to control, I go and get a pistol or, more likely, my old M-1 carbine. And

I head for some safe fields or woods, maybe an abandoned quarry or a dumpsite, and shoot cans and bottles until I am calm again.

Well then.

Thank you for putting up with my monologue.

I challenge, yes I *dare* you to break every general rule I have here asserted.

And good luck be with you.

Shelby Hearon

Shelby Hearon is the author of fourteen novels, including *Footprints, Life Estates,* and *Owning Jolene,* which won an American Academy of Arts and Letters Literature Award. She has received fellowships for fiction from the John Simon Guggenheim Foundation and the National Endowment for the Arts, an Ingram Merrill grant, and has twice won the Texas Institute of Letters fiction award. She has taught in numerous writing programs, and now makes her home in Burlington, Vermont.

Here is as good a sense of the difference between chapters and stories as a starting-out writer is likely to receive.

Letter to Gail Greiner

Gail—

About the story: it just sounds totally like a chapter from a novel. For it to be a short story she and hubby will have to confront about John, Baby will have to find the car, something about Baby finding the car and hubby's salamanders all dying will precipitate a confrontation at the beach which they finally get to, and the universe will never be the same. Whereas, in a novel chapter, she can want the salamanders to die and fall exhausted because tomorrow is another day and THEN the car will appear and THEN the confrontation will take place and THEN we'll learn what hubby confesses AND THEN she'll be preggers again and THEN. . . . Chapters lead on off to the future; story closes up all possible action: Baby never grows older; degree is never received; time freezes. Which is to say, hon, that I wish you'd get back to what you were doing so well, that novel about divorce which the child character was calling DEVORS, which seems to me to rage with life and possibilities.

—Shelby

Janette
Turner Hospital

Janette Turner Hospital is an Australian who grew up on the steamy subtropical coast of Queensland. She began her teaching career in remote parts of her home state, but since her graduate studies she has taught in universities in Australia, Canada, the United States, and England. Her first novel, *The Ivory Swing,* won Canada's Seal First Novel Award. Since then she has won a number of literary prizes for her novels and short-story collections, and her work has been published in ten languages. *Oyster* was short-listed for both of Australia's major literary prizes, the Miles Franklin and the National Book Awards. It was also a finalist for Canada's Trillium Award, and in England it was listed in Best Books of the Year by the *Observer.*

Herewith great advice for a writer who has suffered reversals and knows that it is time to curse fate, and the critics, and then get on with the work.

Letter to a Younger Writer
Met at a Conference

Dear M:

Your letter, full of such pain and confusion, touches me deeply. You wonder if I will remember you, because quite some time has elapsed since we met at a literary conference. You had just been brought from halfway around the world to receive a major short-story award. You blinked in the stage lights, it was your first aria, a handful of publications in little magazines behind you, the draft of a novel in your suitcase.

Do I remember you?

I do indeed; partly, of course, because it was so unexpected to bump into another Australian at a big American event. But also I remember that fog of euphoria and nervousness which surrounded you, the dazed look you had on finding yourself catapulted from the backblocks of the world to a gathering of academics and of writers whose names and works you recognized. You found the scene daunting. (I caught a glimpse of my excited and insecure self of 15 years earlier.) You almost didn't come, you told me. You felt too intimidated. The conference convener had to cajole you by lengthy international phone call.

I remember also the story for which you won the prize. It dazzled me. I remember how the back of my neck prickled as you read it, how I thought with a buzz of excitement: *Here is a voice that is new and powerful and original.* At the time, I asked you for a copy. Now, having received your letter, I've located that copy in my files, and have re-read your story. It still excites me and moves me.

So the very first thing I want to say to you is this: *Hold on to that. Trust your instinct. It gave you your first ticket of leave. Trust it. Trust it.*

We seem to have much in common, you write; and therefore you hope I will understand and advise. Since, as you perceive it, I've weathered a few storms and established a "secure niche" in the literary world, since (as it seems to you, but certainly never to me) I have "achieved success," then I will be able to comfort you in the valley of the shadow of despair and blockage. I will be able to pass on the secret key, the one that unlocks the monstrously heavy vault-like door between paralysis and productivity, darkness and light.

Ah, dear M, comfort I can give freely and abundantly. Advice also, though that is tentative and provisional. But as for the magic key, it is damnably elusive. Sometimes I have it, sometimes not. Sometimes, quite mysteriously, the door simply opens by itself and I'm flooded with light. Sometimes, just as suddenly (if, for example, I've been stupid enough to read a savage review), it slams shut again. But I've found you can go on writing in the dark, and that the act of writing itself, that mysterious, dangerous, intoxicating, absorbing, nourishing magician's trick, that act of creation generates its own light.

I wonder if there's any such thing as a secure niche in the literary world? Perhaps there is; but if so, it would be a deadly thing to achieve in one's lifetime. Smugness and self-satisfaction are surely inimical to art. Certainly no one, least of all Emily Dickinson herself, thought she had achieved any kind of literary status during her lifetime, with only seven poems published, and those anonymously. "Oblivion lingers in the immediate neighborhood," opined the *Atlantic Monthly* when the posthumous collection of her poetry first appeared.

On the other hand, any reading of the complete lists of

Nobel Prize winners, or of American National Book Award winners (or, to be Australian in context, of winners of the Miles Franklin Award) is proof that there is never any shortage of celebrities of brief duration who were thought to have literary immortality in their vest pockets during their lifetimes; and yet it has turned out that their reputations have seeped away like water through sand. The one sure thing about literary immortality is that it can only come posthumously, and even then it can slide up and down the scale, be displaced and replaced. So surely the only thing that should matter is the work in hand.

No matter what the books behind one have achieved in the way of awards and recognition, one starts from scratch with each new act of creation. One puts everything on the line. And why not? Therein lies the pleasure, the addictive risk, the sheer rush of that endorphin high. What would be the point, say, of an Olympic high-jumper re-performing a record jump over and over? How pathetic, tame, boring, embarrassing. She would raise the bar a notch each time, would she not? She would thus increase her chance of failure each time. In my writing, I'm for raising the bar with each novel, each short story. Here's a credo of mine, cribbed from Eugene O'Neill: *Those who succeed and do not push on to greater failure are the spiritual middle-classers.*

You allude to our similarities. We are both very late bloomers who did not begin to publish until after 40, when our children were growing up and in school. We both come from the boondocks, as far from the literary centers of power as it is possible to be, even within our own country, which floats in the Pacific Ocean at a very far remove indeed from New York, London, Paris, those great brokerage houses of the cultural canon. Finally, we were both miraculously catapulted into orbit by winning an international prize before our own country was aware of our literary existence, a phenomenon which has strange consequences for good and ill.

Right now, you feel completely demoralized. You think you will never be able to write again. In the wake of the prize brouhaha, your novel has received some extraordinarily hostile reviews in Australia. And several recent stories, which you feel strongly are the best things you've done, have actually been turned down by literary magazines, and you have become too despondent to send them out again. You have stopped writing. The story which won the prize must have been a lucky fluke, you tell yourself. You're no good. You can't write. You are lost in the dark.

Has this ever happened to me? you ask. Have I ever felt like this?

Answer: yes; several times.

You wonder: Is it to do with your particular situation, because you come from nowhere, have no network of connections in Sydney, New York, wherever? Is it because you are a woman? Australian? A middle-aged beginner? Is it because you were a dark horse who galloped off (perhaps, somehow, illicitly?) with a major prize? Is this the *who the hell is she? who the hell does she think she is?* effect.

Answer: Maybe. It is possible that some or all of those factors have a bearing on the reception of your work; but since there is nothing we can do about such factors, it does not make sense to waste thought or energy on them. They are irrelevant to the matter in hand, which is to recapture your creative energy and self-confidence.

You ask: if I have ever been in such a demoralized state, what did I do?

Answer: The first couple of times, like you, I floundered

around. I bled internally. I walked for miles each day. I spent time in my garden, earth in my hands (the best restorative activity I know of for battered spirits). I read voraciously, I caught up on all the books I'd been meaning to read for years. Even though I knew it was pointless, I began writing anyway, hesitantly, in the dark . . . and then suddenly there I was, writing again, and vibrant.

Since then, I have worked out an emergency drill for bad times. For one thing, I go on compiling my own little list, from my reading, of famous rejections, famous hostile reviews: comic reading for when one's sense of the tragic lurches out of scale. So your best stories have been rejected? Take one sweetmeat from my box, suck slowly, enjoy.

—When Braque submitted his first cubist paintings to the Salon d'Automne in Paris in 1908, they were rejected. He had to show them elsewhere, and the critics—including Matisse—lampooned them.

—Years earlier, Renoir had dismissed the work of Matisse. *Plus ça change* . . .

—When Proust submitted the first sections of *À la Recherche du Temps Perdu* to a publisher, Gide wrote an unfavorable report for Gallimard, who turned down *Swann's Way*.

—The *London Critic* wrote of Walt Whitman's *Leaves of Grass* that "Whitman is as unacquainted with art as a hog is with mathematics."

—Consider the fate of Australia's own Christina Stead, whose books, since her death, are steadily finding their way back into print in multiple languages. She never won a major prize, but when Saul Bellow won his Nobel in 1976, he tipped her as a future winner. No one in Stockholm heard. American critic Randall Jarrell noted, in his introduction to the reissue of *The Man Who Loved Children* (1965), that when the book was first published, in 1940, it "was a failure both with critics and with the public. . . . one of those books that their own age neither reads nor praises, but that the next age thinks is a masterpiece."

And so it goes.

Compile your own list and keep it in a desk drawer. Re-read whenever necessary. Ask yourself: what did Braque, Proust, Whitman, and Stead have in common? They broke the rules. They did something shockingly new. They offended even their own artistic forebears and mentors.

Your writing does that. It startles and disturbs. It violates the taste canons of Sydney and Melbourne, because it knows nothing of them. It has developed in blissful freewheeling isolation on a farm in the scrub at the edge of nowhere, nourished by eclectic and maverick reading not mentioned on current sanctioned lists. Good. Hold on to that prickly uniqueness. Trust it. So you have been reviewed with "extraordinary hostility"? Consider that a good sign. It puts you in very good company.

James Gleick, historian of science, writes in *Chaos:* "Shallow ideas can be assimilated. Ideas that require people to reorganize their picture of the world provoke hostility."

"Only he writes well who has the courage to break the rules," declared Tuscan poet Angelo Poliziano, in rebellion against the slavish imitation of antiquity. That was in 1491.

Keep these citations at your side, like talismans to be fondled, if you must read your hostile reviews. Better not to, of course, though early in one's career it can be difficult to resist the morbid fascination. It's a bad habit that one quickly outgrows, but until then, chew reviews fast then spit them out, and above all, never attempt to cut your cloth to please your critics. That way lies sure and certain artistic self-mutilation.

I must also warn you, however, that in one year, or five, your judgment of this same novel may well be harsher than that of your nastiest critic. We become tougher with ourselves. There is always a gap between conception and execution. We keep writing in the burning hope of closing that gap before we die.

So there is my emergency kit drill in a nutshell:

1) Take time out to comfort and console yourself
2) Trust your instincts
3) Be defiant (and nurture the defiant streak by reading biographies of writers, painters, composers; by going to concerts and art galleries)
4) Be your own most exigent critic
5) Start writing in the dark if you have to

To students, I have been known to put this more flippantly and more succinctly. When rejection slips or rotten reviews come in, I tell them: have one stiff drink, say five Hail Mary's and ten Fuck-You's, and get back to work.

You mention other peripheral anxieties in passing; and compared with staying the course and keeping the creative engines ticking over, these issues are indeed peripheral. How does one survive financially by one's writing? In my experience, one doesn't. Of course, I know that a lucky few do; but most don't. So far, in spite of nine books, prizes, and multiple translations, I have earned writing income adequate for survival in only a few years, and those were not, alas, the most recent years. It has been a bit of a blow to find that my income can regress. Maybe it will rise again. If so, that will be wonderful. If not, so what? I teach when I can, but I have also, of necessity, had to scramble to do many other things to survive, from sweat-shop garment work to selling mutual funds for a financial institution. (Good literary precedent there; Eliot worked in a bank, remember?) These non-literary and non-academic pursuits, while not paying well, are nevertheless worth their weight in narrative gold.

What about grants? you ask. I know many writers who have had them, and who swear by them. I know many others who have become embittered (very bad for one's writing) because they applied but did not receive. I never apply. My personal recommendation is: don't waste your time, because the grant system (in whatever country) fosters cultural politicking, backscratching, mutual favoritisms, bitterness, and a host of other noxious syndromes that sap at the only kind of energy that matters, which is your itch to create. Get yourself whatever regular employment and income you can, it does not matter what it is, so long as it allows you to structure writing time into your life. No one owes us writers a living, certainly not our fellow taxpayers—not that I would recommend looking a gift horse in the mouth if one were to come nuzzling you and offering to sponsor a year of writing time. In that case, accept with gratitude. There is no question one is more productive when one has time to write and freedom from financial anxiety. But what we do, we do because it is our own passionate and pleasurable compulsion. We should organize our lives to support our own addiction, because we are the lucky ones, the gloriously self-indulgent, the self-annointed, and what can possibly be compared with that rush, the fondling of words, the creation of a world *ex nihilo,* the god-itch, the spinning of gold from the straw-shop of our minds?

As for me, when the spinning-wheel flags or jams, I go cruising. I cruise bars, the subway, art galleries. Especially art galleries. I look at paintings and sculptures. I read the diaries and letters and lives of the painters. Perhaps it is the very tangibility, the concreteness, of their acts of creation; perhaps it is because the medium is altogether different from mine, and therefore my reaction is direct and uncomplicated. Whatever the reason, some sort of crackling energy leaps across the gap from the mind of the painter to mine. I catch fire. I go home and write. My writing has nothing whatsoever to do with the paintings themselves. There is no symbolic link. It is simply free-floating verve which zaps me. Certain exhibitions continue to cast an aura of energy for years afterwards. I have just to close my eyes and think of them again, or browse the catalogs. I can tie one of my novels like a tail to the comet of the Brancusi exhibition in Paris in '95, and short stories trail the "Late Braque" in London in '97, and "Picasso—the early years" in Boston last year.

"I live with Goya," Picasso told André Malraux in a 1944 interview. "I paint against the canvases that are important to me, but I paint in accord with everything that's still missing . . ."

Those words never fail to excite me. I pass them on to you. Go on writing what is still missing from the literary tradition. Go on breaking rules. Go on provoking hostility.

Write in the dark for a while if you have to, and put on your old *Abbey Road* tape while you do it. Listen to the Beatles belting out *"Here Comes the Sun."*

All my very best wishes,
Janette Turner Hospital

Lewis Lapham

An award-winning writer of essays about American culture, the author of six books, Lapham is the editor of *Harper's* magazine.

His warning about the writing profession will strike echoes within those who have, in spite of similar warnings, stuck to their last.

Ars longa, vita brevis

20 September 1997
Little Marsh Farm
Devon, Pennsylvania

Dear Graydon,

I thought we had finished with the subject of you wanting to become a writer when you passed through New York last April en route to your mother's wedding in Venice. You asked for what you called "an uncle's meddling advice," and we spent the better part of an afternoon at a bar on East 10th Street, talking about your chances of commercial or critical success (nil and next to none), about the number of readers that constitutes the American audience for literature (not enough to fill the seats at Yankee Stadium), about the Q-ratings awarded to authors by the celebrity markets (equivalent to those assigned to trick dogs and retired generals), about the consolations of art (enjoyed posthumously). You didn't disagree with the drift of the conversation, and I thought it was understood that you would apply to business school or pursue the chance of an offer from your friend at Microsoft.

Now I'm told that after you graduate from Stanford next spring you mean to work the Alaskan salmon runs for six months and then travel for two years with a Navajo rock band, gathering notes for the great American road novel. Your mother and I had dinner last night in Philadelphia, and she presented me with your August manifesto, the one in which you describe California as a "desert of materialism" and declare your release from the prison of "store-bought, prerecorded dreams." I'm not sure that I can properly describe your mother's mood. Worried and depressed, but at the same time furious—with your stupidity, my complacence, the mediocrity of the restaurant (not up to the standard to which she's become accustomed in Europe), the day of the week, her nail polish, and the rain. Her questions were mostly rhetorical, asked in a tone of voice with which I'm sure you're familiar:

"Doesn't he know what century he's living in, for God's sake? Has he no sense of what things cost? No ambition? No wish to know the important people in the world?"

No matter how often I explained that I'd made more or less the same points when you and I discussed the prospect of your literary career last spring in Greenwich Village, she refused to be comforted.

"Yes," she said, "but you also told him he had talent . . . that his stories showed signs of promise. You're his only uncle, the only male relative he still trusts, the only person he knows who writes books. What did you expect him to think? That your opinion doesn't count? That you were being supportive and polite, like one of those moth-eaten English professors who discover the mark of genius in any student capable of using the word 'ambiguity' twice in the same paragraph?"

I wasn't being polite, Graydon. Both the stories that you published in the Stanford *Chaparral* show a good deal more promise than most of the fiction that appears in *The New Yorker*, but I shouldn't have said so, and I hope that you will forgive my carelessness. You have a talent for literary expression, but when matched against the trend and spirit of the times it's a superfluous talent—like playing the harpsichord or shooting the Plains buffalo. Amuse yourself with literature when you're older than whoever happens to be president of the United States or rich enough to acquire *The Sewanee Review*. In the meantime, learn to buy hotels.

Before coming to the dessert (a chocolate mousse that your mother pronounced "acceptable") I managed to mollify her with the promise to once again impose upon your patience the wisdom of Polonius. She seemed pleased by my saying that the rock band probably would disintegrate before you boarded the bus in Tucson, but she telephoned the next day from Dulles Airport, reminding me to remind you that she no longer has any appreciable money of her own and that she cannot ask Guelpho to sponsor your literary apprenticeship.

Guelpho apparently hasn't forgiven you for the toast that you proposed at his wedding. ("To my mother's fifth husband, Count Guelpho Faranelli, may he pass and be forgotten with the rest.") Guelpho understands that you were drunk at the time, and it has been explained to him that you intended a complex irony (the jewel of flattery concealed in the glove of insult), but he is not well-versed in the forms of American humor. Neither is he a reader of Flaubert's novels or an admirer of Chekhov's plays. A proud aristocrat, Graydon, who nevertheless yearns to hear you praise his collection of Roman portrait busts and his mastery of the Argentine tango. Antonio Banderas once told him that never in his life had he seen so heavy a man so delicately execute the *paseo de la muerte*. The count cherishes the remark.

It's conceivable, of course, that your manifesto was another complex irony meant to frighten your mother (in the way that boys of your age and disposition sometimes threaten to enlist in the marines or marry a rodeo star), and maybe, like Guelpho, I've failed to guess your intention. But in the event that you might mean at least some of what you say, and by way of making good on my promise to your mother, allow me to review the argument.

The existence of a literature presupposes a literate and coherent public that has both the time to read and a need to take seriously the works of the literary imagination. I'm not sure whether the United States ever had such a public; certainly it hasn't had one for the last thirty years. What we have instead is an opening-night crowd, astonished by celebrity and opulent spectacle, tolerating only those authors who present themselves as freaks and wonders and offer the scandal of their lives as proof of their art. Lacking even one critic whose judgment means anything, the management of the nation's literary affairs falls naturally into the hands of accountants and press agents—i.e., life-forms native to "the deserts of materialism."

Walk into the brightly packaged clutter of the nearest bookstore, and what do you see? Mostly what you would see in *The National Enquirer* or on *Entertainment Tonight*—movie-star gossip, secrets of the pyramids and the stock market, guides to better health, confessions of accomplished swindlers and convicted murderers, beauty tips from notorious madams, the latest bulletins updating the E.T.A. for the end of the world.

If you've been reading the papers, you will have noticed that the publishing business lately has fallen upon hard times. This year's sales for adult trade books (the category you intend to make the canvas of your ambition) have dropped by 12 percent; the bookstores keep new books on their shelves for about the same length of time (five days, maybe two weeks) that grocers keep light cream and sun-dried tomatoes, and they return unsold books to their points of origin at the rate of 45 percent. Which is why even the most literate publishers (the ones who remember that F. Scott Fitzgerald died of drink) seldom take chances with commodities that fail to meet the standards of tabloid journalism and why their best-selling authors turn out to be the kind of people apt to require the services of a capable bail bondsman. When signing the contracts and arranging the publicity, nobody raises a glass of sherry to the memory of Maxwell Perkins. The more subtle the author's thought and the more careful his argument, the smaller his chance of notice. Not enough people will understand what he's trying to say. The shoddy work sells as well as, or better than, the good work, and why confuse the computers in charge of sales with anything other than "store-bought, prerecorded dreams"?

Even those authors whom you admire and presumably consider serious cannot escape the burden of mechanical repetition. Who among them can afford to take chances with a $400,000 advance against royalties and the good opinion of the lecture bureaus? Unless they say what they said last time, how can they become reliable products? The transformation of subject into object serves the interest of the market, but it is a bargain that tends to rob writers of their courage.

If you were a young Englishman at large in the streets of Elizabethan London (an impoverished scholar, say, without land, title, or acquaintance in court), you might have tried your luck as a poet or a playwright. It was an age that delighted in the rush of words to which we now affix the seals and stamps of literature. Conceivably you could have made your way into the circle of patronage surrounding Sir Walter Raleigh or Lord Strange. You might also have been imprisoned for sedition or hanged as a spy, but on the way to the scaffold you at least would have known that you had walked, if only briefly, on the world's stage and that the queen's ministers thought well enough of your wit to kill you for the crime of a well-turned phrase.

So, too, in the nineteenth century, whether in Europe or on the East Coast of America, authors of note commanded the attention of princes and the adulation of the mob. Lord Byron's contemporaries trembled at the approach of his verses; Dickens lectured to crowds not unlike those that now attend concerts by Garth Brooks; all of Boston wept in the presence of Emerson's sermons; Victor Hugo could have been elected president of France.

During the first half of the twentieth century the figure of the literary hero retained an aura of power and authority—think of James Joyce, of Thomas Mann, or Ernest Hemingway as *The Old Man and the Sea*—but the role has been rendered irrelevant by television and the hydrogen bomb, reduced to farce by Norman Mailer's traipsing around the department-store book-signing circuit dressed up in the persona of King Lear.

The literary crowd likes to mourn the death of the written word and regret the disappearance of "public intellectuals" who supposedly once led the readers of American newspapers, like a flock of confused sheep, into the pastures of enlightenment. The familiar dirge can be best understood as advertising promotion. It isn't that the modern world has abandoned the written word but rather that certain kinds of literary usage or construction have lost their currency and force. The surge of human intellect always flows into the sea of public event, but in the late twentieth century the rivers of expression drain the uplands of the sciences and the watersheds of the film and computer technologies. People ask the questions they deem important (What is man? Why do I have to die?) not of poets or novelists but of chemists and cosmetic surgeons.

HBO and prime-time television offer the rewards of both fame and fortune that long ago and once upon a time attracted the Cambridge wits to the Elizabethan stage, and were Shakespeare now alive on St. Crispin's Day you could expect to find him arranging the play of light and shadow in a Hollywood movie studio. A Wall Street investment bank composes a seventeen-page prospectus laying out the plot for the merger of two pharmaceutical companies, and its author's fee comes up to an amount (maybe $4 million, possibly as much as $10 million) that dwarfs the earnings of all the books enrolled on any season's bestseller list. The sums that large corporations routinely allot every year to upgrading their communications systems exceed, by a multiple of four, the annual subsidies grudgingly donated to the National Endowments for the Humanities and the Arts. I've known lawyers to compose trust agreements with as many tiers of hidden meaning as can be found in Herman Melville's chapter on the whiteness of Moby Dick.

Last winter when the Clinton Administration identified the 831 guests who had stayed overnight in the White House, did you see the names of any writers on the list? Steven Spielberg dropped by, and so did Barbra Streisand and Tom Hanks, but where was Thomas Pynchon? The President has seen *High Noon* no fewer than twenty times. How many times do you think he's read *The Crying of Lot 49?* I don't wish to bore you with the obvious, Graydon, but when have you seen a writer on a golf course with Michael Jordan, on the screen with Ted Koppel, on the cover of *Vanity Fair?*

Which is, I think, your mother's principal objection to your thesis of a literary career. Where's the glamour in it? The hope of adventure? The chance of an appearance in the gossip columns? Within the ghetto of the literary life, the money is small, the accommodations poor, the circle of acquaintance necessarily limited (like that of a motorcycle or kennel club), the conversation paranoid, the people almost never pretty.

Your mother tends to exaggerate the importance of appearances (one of her traits of character that both of us must hope Count Faranelli finds endearing), and when she speaks of writers as persons uniformly "sallow, bitter, self-preoccupied, envious, furtive, and drab," she overstates her point. It's not true that all writers lurk in corners gnawing on old cocktail cheese. I've known writers who dine on pheasant. Some of them stand in the center of the room. A few of them write remarkable books.

But neither is your mother entirely wrong. Why squander your talent and intelligence on a career that leads, even under the best of circumstances, nowhere but into the footnoted gloom of one of the country's neo-Gothic universities? Fast-forward the calendar to the year 2027 and grant yourself the unlikely favor of literary success—the author of four novels critically acclaimed on three continents (none of which sold more than 15,000 copies in hardcover and 40,000 in paper), celebrated by *Newsweek* as "the poet of despair" and by *Time* as "the conscience of the age," writer in residence at Duke, occasional but esteemed contributor to *The New York Review of Books,* sought after by the sponsors of summer creative-writing programs, the lion of Bread Loaf—groomed by librarians, cosseted by graduate students, fed from the dish of foundation grants.

All well and good and devoutly to be wished, but to what purpose? Books have so little to do with the business of America that the writers who aspire to the status of literary trademarks reserve their most vivid narratives to the story of the self. But if it is the life and not the book that becomes the work of art, why go to the intermediate trouble of constructing sentences instead of leveraged-buyout deals?

Become a partner at Salomon Brothers, write episodes of *Seinfeld* or jokes for David Letterman, speculate on the Shanghai Stock Exchange, sell music videos to the Russians, curry favor with George Soros, but keep thy foot out of English departments and flee the company of young women familiar with the names of Joseph Conrad and Marcel Proust.

Work the Alaskan salmon run or wander with the Navajo, but do so because you wish to travel, not because you plan to write a book. Make the mistake of thinking that you can decide to become a writer and you've already lost the bet. Writers happen by accident, not by design. They have as little choice in the matter as lemmings toppling over cliffs. If and when the spirit moves you (and you find yourself being drawn irretrievably to the sea), it won't occur to you to ask or heed anybody's advice, least of all that of

> your fond and word-ridden uncle,
> Dyer

Stanley W. Lindberg

Since 1977, Lindberg has edited *The Georgia Review* and has, therefore, helped—according to this book's editor—to shape American writing from Athens, Georgia, as well as from Athens, Ohio, where, from 1970 to 1977, he was cofounder of, and editor with, the *Ohio Review*. He has received editing awards from the American Society of Magazine Editors, the Coordinating Council of Literary Magazines, and the National Endowment for the Arts. He is the author of *The Annotated McGuffey, Van Nostrand's Plain English Handbook,* and *The Legacy of Erskine Caldwell*. He is coauthor of *The Nature of Copyright* and has coedited two literary anthologies, *Necessary Fictions* and *Keener Sounds*. He was the first recipient of the Georgia Governor's Award in the Humanities.

An encouragement, and a reminder about the dues a writer must pay.

But before You Start . . .

28 July 1998

Dear Joel,

I was not at all surprised to learn that you've decided to pursue writing seriously, and I certainly wish you all the best toward that worthy end. Although you've sent me little of your recent work, the stories you sent me last Christmas demonstrated both talent and promise—I wouldn't have encouraged you then if I'd thought otherwise—so I'm far less distressed now than you are over Iowa's decision not to accept you into their MFA program. Your disappointment is understandable, of course, but their action "rejected" only your candidacy this year—not you—and your situation is far from catastrophic. Indeed, I'm willing to bet that eventually you'll come to view this temporary setback as for the best— in both the short *and* the long run.

So, you say you want to be an author, and you've asked for some pointers to help get your career "back on track." I'm going to take you at your word, Joel, and try to share here some of what I've learned in almost thirty years as an editor. But I'll give you fair warning before we start: I'll probably be dishing out more realism here than you expect. (I figure you already have enough idealism for both of us at this point, so I won't be pulling punches.) Nothing I say should be taken as gospel, however— mine is just one truck driver's opinion—and if anything here surprises you or conflicts with what others have advised, you'll have to decide how much weight to give it. Obviously I hope you'll find something of value in my comments, but in the end you need to trust your own instincts. Remember, no one can write for you—it's up to you to make something of yourself—so don't do anything just to please me or anyone else.

200

Let's go over some fundamentals, starting with your request itself. I know you're too smart to expect me to specify a guaranteed "career track" to success—such doesn't exist, has never existed. But it's really not very healthy for you (and definitely premature at this early stage of your life) to be talking about a career as an author. Careers are not roles one can just step into; they have to be earned, sometimes developing in ways that surprise even their possessors—especially those who thought they knew exactly what they were going after. (My own experience serves as one example: I have always loved literature, but I never set out to work with contemporary creative writing as the editor of *The Georgia Review*. I wrote my dissertation on Dr. Samuel Johnson, expecting to specialize in teaching 18th-century British literature.) At this stage in your life you should be concentrating on making yourself the best person and best writer you can be, rather than worrying about designating a specific career and trying to fit yourself into that mold.

For what it's worth, Joel, you should know that the majority of writers in America are unable to support themselves solely by their efforts as writers. I'm certainly not trying to discourage you from your chosen path or persuade you to enter the business world—and I can only laugh at your light-hearted assurance that you "don't expect to earn as much right away as Stephen King and John Grisham do." It's a damned good thing that you don't! But I suspect that you hold a fairly unrealistic idea as to *how much* less than such best-selling storytellers your writing is likely to earn for many years. In truth, Joel, if you feel compelled to write and are really serious in your pursuit, you had better find something (or, if you're lucky, *someone*) to pay the bills while you are learning your trade. When we read headlines about the enormous advances extended to a very few writers, it's all too easy for any of us to imagine reaping a similar harvest—and to start thinking along the lines of "Actually, I could get through the year on only 10% of an advance that size—maybe I should take less up front and insist on retaining film rights." Obviously it would be a wonderful world if such romantic fantasies came true for someone as nice as you, but don't spend that windfall money until you're sure it's in hand.

More troubling to me than such wishful thinking, however, is your repeated desire to become an "author." Authors, Joel, are published *writers,* and I know of very few (excluding politicians and celebrities who employ ghostwriters on their behalf) who earned the label without a hell of a lot of hard work. So, stop thinking of becoming an *author*—that is, stop negotiating imaginary contracts, basking in media spotlights, signing books you've yet to write for your thousands of adoring fans—and work instead to become a *writer.* You've garnered some prizes so far, and you've received nice comments and recommendations from teachers and others sensitive to your self-esteem, but the rest of the world is going to expect more tangible accomplishments before encouraging you to feel good about yourself as a writer. And if you think I'm being too rough on you here, either thicken your skin or brace yourself for when reality hits.

The last time we talked, you seemed somewhat embarrassed when I asked what jobs you had held over the years. Actually I hadn't expected you to have had a lot before college—life as a teenager today can be quite full with music lessons, soccer, cross country, etc—but you may recall that I raised an eyebrow when your work record during college turned out to be pretty thin, too. (I was not, by the way, introducing the question as part of a character analysis. I was curious as to the variety of experiences you had to draw upon—and how they might enrich your writing.) Jobs can do more than put bread on the table, Joel. They can extend and deepen your education by furnishing you an unending supply of rich characters, moments that excite or move you, observations of cruel injustices that you are powerless to rectify, stretches of incredible boredom, temptations of many varieties, frustrations, close friendships, inexplicably malignant behavior, motives and plots more complex than any you have previously imagined.

Such employment "bonuses"—as well as honest sweat, tears, rage, and a frequent, overwhelming urge to shitcan all such educational enrichments—can be invaluable in helping you ground yourself as a writer and to find focus and substance. To be sure, solipsistic angst by itself can generate enough fodder to win undergraduate literary prizes (and still informs fiction in some slick magazines), but you'll soon find that only an immense talent can stretch it very far. Learn to look *outside* of yourself—and learn to imagine yourself *inside* someone else's life and problems. Until you've experienced life away from the artificiality of academe and can weave concrete elements convincingly into your storytelling, you'll find that not many readers (excluding your good parents, of course) will find your interior monologues very compelling. And to paraphrase the wise philosopher Yogi Berra, if the reading public wants to stay away in droves, you can't stop 'em—or the editors and publishers who will look elsewhere to fill their pages and satisfy their readers.

What I'm about to say now may seem harsh, Joel, although I certainly don't intend it to be, and I hope you'll understand. Try to step back and take an objective look at the writing samples you submitted in your application to Iowa. Can you see how dominant the first-person singular pronoun is in your writing, how the inner conflicts tend to float, deeply absorbed with self but essentially unanchored? Rather than three separate stories, they could easily be read as nicely turned variations on a single theme. Such a summary may do them an injustice, Joel, but I want you to realize how much these selections stay on a single tonal trajectory, lacking variety or surprise in subject or technique. Those characteristics—and the lack of concrete referents—may very well have been factors arguing against your getting into the Iowa Writers Workshop on the first try. Competition for spots in that distinguished program has always been keen, with some of the applicants being writers who have been working in the profession for several years. Not only are such candidates more experienced in life than you (and most others just graduating from college), their writing is likely to be significantly more mature. I'd be surprised, in fact, if most of those admitted this year did *not* already have publication credits *beyond* being in their college literary magazines. In short, they have done more than you to earn that admission.

Fortunately, it's now totally up to you as to whether or not you choose to do what they did. Some mighty fine writers never took a creative writing course, but if you still want to study at Iowa or in some other graduate writing program— and there are *many* other fine programs around the country to consider—you can set yourself to work, strengthen your credentials, and apply again. In the meantime, however, get a job in the real world and start writing something every day— after work or early every morning. Carry a notebook and use spare moments (even at work, if you can get away with it) to capture the description of something, wrestle with an idea, explore a character, a mood, whatever. Put aside for now your dreams of being an author and work instead to become a writer—a far more worthy objective.

Oh yes, and you should read. Read the literature you never got around to when it was recommended in the past by your friends and former teachers—and to educate yourself in other ways, read also some worthy books on the bestseller lists. Read poetry and essays, not just the fiction, in a variety of literary journals and magazines. Read for enjoyment—and always with an eye to learn from other writers' skills. Read biographies and histories. Read book reviews and discover which reviewers you tend to trust—and why. Read.

You may have heard some writers claim that they never read anyone else's work while they are busy on a project of their own—they don't want another voice breaking in, they fear another's influence, etc. I bring this up not to debate such reasoning but because I've actually heard some younger writers using the "I don't want to contaminate my originality" excuse for not reading the work of others *at all*—a self-limiting policy that I urge you to reject totally. Read as much as you can of Dickens and Twain and Chekhov—and other authors you've never before made enough time to read. But check out also James Joyce and Eudora Welty, Kafka and Hemingway, Faulkner and Virginia Woolf. And don't stop there. After you survey as many different contemporary quarterlies and literary magazines as you can—reading for *breadth*—then single out the contemporary writers you find most engaging, get their books, and start to read for *depth*.

A good library offers a feast of free reading, of course, but please don't feel you need to wait for the library to buy or subscribe to everything you're anxious to read. Few would dispute that most would-be writers find cash a scarce commodity, but if you honestly intend to enter this profession, you ought to participate in the literary economy to the extent that you can. No one expects you to subscribe to all the journals and magazines you want to submit work to, but if you can afford to buy a new CD to listen to or a case of beer for a party, you ought to be able to budget *something* for subscriptions and book purchases. If you expect your favorite literary magazine still to be there when you are ready to publish in it, maybe you ought to help ensure that possibility by subscribing to it. If you admire a particular author's work and hope to see more, dig deep and cast your economic vote by buying his or her latest novel.

Enough for now. That's far more advice than you bargained for, and it's probably not what you expected. If you were hoping for a line-by-line critique of your writing or for more detailed suggestions regarding how to get it published, I'm sorry to have disappointed you. I believe we'll have plenty of time later to deal with those matters. There's no need for you to rush into print now. At this point, in my opinion, it's far more important for you to learn and build on your strengths as a writer, to get involved with life, and to find the stories that you feel *need* to be told. Then—after you've written those stories, telling each one as well as you can—we can talk about publishing.

In writing, only results count—not authorial intent or anguish, not the number of hours spent at the desk—and you will have to learn to live with and overcome failures along the way. When you start to get discouraged, Joel, keep in mind that our society makes multimillionaires out of baseball players who fail utterly seven times out of every ten trips to the plate. Do not, however, take too much comfort in that bit of wisdom. For one thing, major leaguers—even those on "base salary"—eat very well, whereas writers on minimum wage can be found asking people if they want ketchup with their fries. For another, you'll find that batting .300 anytime is more difficult than it looks—especially as you move up to the bigger leagues. But keep on trying, and learn from the negative experiences that are inevitable. If a magazine declines your offer to grace its pages with one of your stories, don't take it as a personal rejection. Try to connect somewhere else, and/or try to make your stories more compelling. I think you can make yourself a fine writer, Joel, but my opinion really doesn't matter. It's up to you.

Yr Editor in Waiting

Joyce Carol Oates

Joyce Carol Oates is the author most recently of the novel *My Heart Laid Bare,* the story collection *The Collector of Hearts,* and *Where I've Been, and Where I'm Going: Essays, Reviews and Prose.* Her first children's book, *Come Meet Muffin!,* has recently been published, and she is the editor of *Telling Stories: A Reader for Writers* (Norton). She teaches at Princeton University and is a member of the American Academy of Arts and Letters.

An eminent writer in full stride advises someone starting out about those early, faltering steps.

To a Young Writer

To a Young Writer:

> All that a man has to say or do that can possibly concern mankind, is in some shape or other to tell the story of his love,—to sing; and, if he is fortunate and keeps alive, he will be forever in love. This alone is to be alive to the extremities.
>
> —Henry David Thoreau, Journal, 6 May 1854

(Yet keep in mind Thoreau's other, more sardonic aside in the first chapter of *Walden:*

> I have lived some thirty years on this planet, and I have yet to hear the first syllable of valuable or even earnest advice from my seniors. They have told me nothing, and probably cannot tell me anything, to the purpose. Here is life, an experiment . . . untried by me; but it does not avail me that they have tried it . . . One generation abandons the enterprises of another like stranded vessels.

How achingly true this seemed to me when I was a young, adolescent writer, and seems so still!)

If it's your ambiguous destiny to be a writer, you already know that no one can tell you what to do; how to behave; still less how to think, and how to feel about yourself. At the most you can acquire from others an "external self"—a mode of being that allows you to seem to conform while releasing you, in your imagination, to whatever adventures await you. The experience of writing is primarily an *adventure,* not a vocation; if it feels like destiny and not choice, you should understand at the start that it's as likely to be a curse as a blessing, and while rejoicing in a surpassingly beautiful work of art may be a benefit of civilization, it is one possibly not experienced by the creator of that work of art him- or herself.

Transcribing visions into language, giving a form and structure to the imagination within, is a self-consuming activity. Each work you create exacts a price from you, in proportion to its worth to you. To be a writer—or any kind of "creative" artist, as opposed to an artist-for-hire (which may be a perfectly honest and legitimate vocation)—is to plunge into the unknown that lies within. The exterior or social self is a shell that can protect or stifle you depending upon the accident of circumstances.

Write your heart out.

Never be ashamed of your subject, and of your passion for your subject.

Your "forbidden" passions are likely to be the fuel for your writing. Like our great American dramatist Eugene O'Neill raging through his life against a long-deceased father; like our great American prose stylist Ernest Hemingway raging through his life against his mother; like Sylvia Plath and Anne Sexton struggling through their lives with the seductive Angel of Death, tempting them to the ecstasy of self-murder. The instinct for violent self-laceration in Dostoyevsky, and for the sadistic punishment of "disbelievers" in Flannery O'Connor. The fear of going mad in Edgar Allan Poe and committing an irrevocable, unspeakable act—murdering an elder or a wife, hanging and putting out the eyes of one's "beloved" pet cat. Your struggle with your buried self, or selves, yields your art; these emotions are the fuel that drives your writing and makes possible hours, days, weeks, months and years of what will appear to others, at a distance, as "work." Without these ill-understood drives you might be a superficially happier person, and a more involved citizen of your community, but it isn't likely that you will create anything of substance.

What advice can an older writer presume to offer to a younger? Only what he or she might wish to have been told years ago. Don't be discouraged! Don't cast sidelong glances, and compare yourself to others among your peers! (Writing is not a race. No one really "wins." The satisfaction is in the effort, and rarely in the consequent rewards, if there are any.) And again, *write your heart out.*

Read widely, and without apology. Read what you want to read, not what someone tells you you should read. (As Hamlet remarks, "I know not 'should.' ") Immerse yourself in a writer you love, and read everything he or she has written, including the very earliest work. Especially the very earliest work. Before the great writer became great, or even good, he/she was groping for a way, fumbling to acquire a voice, perhaps just like you.

Write for your own time, if not for your own generation exclusively. You can't write for "posterity"—it doesn't exist. You can't write for a departed world. You may be addressing, unconsciously, an audience that doesn't exist; you may be trying to please someone who won't be pleased, and who isn't worth pleasing.

(But if you feel unable to "write your heart out"—inhibited, embarrassed, fearful of hurting or offending the feelings of others—you may want to try a practical solution and write under a pseudonym. There's something wonderfully liberating, even childlike, about a "pen-name": a fictitious name given to the instrument with which you write, and not attached to *you*. If your circumstances change, you could always claim your writing self. You could always abandon your writing self, and cultivate another. Early publication can be a dubious blessing: we all know writers who would give anything to have not published their first book, and go about trying to buy up all existing copies. Too late!)

(Of course, if you want a professional life that involves teaching, lectures, readings—you will have to acknowledge a public writing name. But only *one*.)

Don't expect to be treated justly by the world. Don't even expect to be treated mercifully.

Life is lived head-on, like a roller coaster ride; "art" is coolly selective, and can be created only in retrospect. But don't live life in order to write about it since the "life" so lived will be artificial and pointless. Better to invent wholly an alternate life. Far better!

Most of us fall in love with works of art, many times during the course of our lifetimes. Give yourself up in admiration, even in adoration, of another's art. (How Degas worshipped Manet! How Melville loved Hawthorne! And how many young, yearning, brimming-with-emotion poets has Walt Whitman sired!) If you find an exciting, arresting, disturbing voice or vision, immerse yourself in it. You will learn from it. In my life I've fallen in love with (and never wholly fallen out of love from) writers as diverse as Lewis Carroll, Emily Brontë, Kafka, Poe, Melville, Emily Dickinson, William Faulkner, Charlotte Brontë, Dostoyevsky . . . In reading the new edition of Mark Twain's *Huckleberry Finn* not long ago, I discovered I'd memorized entire passages of this novel. In rereading the now virtually unread Studs Lonigan trilogy, by James T. Farrell, I discovered I'd memorized entire passages. There are poems of Emily Dickinson I probably know more intimately than Emily Dickinson herself knew them; they are imprinted in my memory in a way they would not have been imprinted in hers. There are poems of William Butler Yeats, Walt Whitman,

Robert Frost, D. H. Lawrence that leave me chilled with excitement decades after I'd first discovered them.

Don't be ashamed of being an idealist, of being romantic and "yearning." If you yearn for people who won't reciprocate your interest in them, you should know that your yearning for them is probably the most valuable thing about them. So long as it's unrequited.

Don't too quickly prejudge classics. Or contemporaries. Choose a book to read, now and then, against the grain of your taste, or what you believe is your taste. It *is* a man's world; a woman whose sensibility has been stoked by feminism will find much to annoy and offend, but perhaps there's much to learn, and to be inspired by, if only in knowing what it is to be an outsider gazing in. Such great works as Homer's *Odyssey* and Ovid's *Metamorphoses,* read from the perspective of the twenty-first century, the one primitive in its genius, the other unnervingly "modern," strike male and female readers in very different ways. A woman should acknowledge her hurt, her anger and her hope of "justice"; even a hope for revenge might be a good thing, in her work if not in her life.

Language is an icy-cool medium, on the page. Unlike performers and athletes, we get to re-imagine, revise and rewrite completely if we wish. Before our work is set *in print,* as *in stone,* we maintain our power over it. The first draft may be stumbling and exhausting, but the next draft or drafts will be soaring and exhilarating. Only have faith: the first sentence can't be written until the last sentence has been written. Only then do you know where you've been going, and where you've been.

The novel is the affliction for which only the novel is the cure.

And one final time: *Write your heart out.*

Reynolds Price

His first novel, *A Long and Happy Life,* was published in 1962, beginning one of the most productive American literary careers. A child of
the South and a writer about its people, Price creates characters who
have stepped away from their region and even from his stories and
novels; like Rosacoke Mustian of his first novel or the eponymous
Kate Vaiden, they have become prized, known, and lived among by
Price's readers. His meditations, essays, plays, poems, and translations, as well as these fictive characters, are the work of an important and importantly religious writer.

*Price here breaks the bad news to someone
who might think to emulate him.*

Letter to a Young Writer

Dear ———,

If you can stop, you probably should. Try cabinet-making, try building fine musical instruments (clavichords or Celtic harps), try forestry—any trade in which you can work in brief solitude, at natural speeds, and for which there is at least a steady demand, however small. If you persist in writing novels, stories, poems, plays, you will almost certainly work in long solitude with no materials but the fragile contents of your own unconscious, many of which are irreplaceable; and you will be stunned to find that the demand for your artifacts is extremely small.

As an American, you have grown up in a society with an apparently inexhaustible taste for music and narrative. Forget music (your *verbal* music requires a great deal more in the way of strenuous cooperation from the audience than any song with instrumental accompaniment). Ah, but narrative, you're thinking—surely I can fill a small portion of the vast and ceaseless craving for *story* that continues to move the American public.

Wrong, probably. If you concentrate on fiction—and on relatively traditional, realistic, chronologically consecutive accounts of the lives of at least partially sympathetic characters—and if you're very good at the craft, then you may well accumulate a loyal audience of five to twenty thousand buyers (there will be other readers of borrowed copies and perhaps even of a paperback edition, but I'm talking here of what you can hope to count on—a first trade-edition, in whose manufacture and proofreading you've had at least the role of adviser). If you're writing poems—again, accessible to readers of a fairly normal taste and training—you may realistically expect, say, three thousand buyers. Beyond those rough certainties, you are casting your bread endlessly upon unfathomable waters; and you must not await its return.

Why? Because you will be offering bread for which—however great you may think the *need*—there is precious little demand. Without going into the large question of why "serious" writing has been increasingly estranged from popular audiences (or whether it has, whether there were ever sizable audiences for serious work), the explanation for the present small demand would seem to be simple—only a tiny group in any population will wish to turn, in its leisure time, to an activity as relentless in its own requirements as the reading of a truthful novel or poem. You will be asking, unavoidably, too much. To acknowledge the fact is to imply no automatic contempt for whole populations. Most people lead lives which they perceive as hard; in their moments of freedom, they are not likely to choose further degrees of hardness—a performance of, say, *King Lear* or *Endgame,* an evening alone with the poems of Robert Lowell, a novel by Robert Stone, or James Welch. The fact that a few hundred or thousand people do make such choices does not automatically attest to their personal virtue. Such a belief continues to poison considerable numbers of American writers, young and old.

There are other serious impediments. The dire fate of serious prose-fiction and verse in the hands of many trade-publishers is widely understood, and there is little point in reciting again the classic litany of horror—volumes that were pulped a few days before winning the Pulitzer, the universal cry of "No advertising," the by-now expected bolloxing of simple matters of distribution (that have long ago been solved by most other brands of American business), the abandonment of a young or old writer whose widely praised work has not met commercial standards appropriate only in a Book Utopia, the increasing indifference of both trade and paperback houses to serious work. My own twenty-year experience of trade publishing has been fairly lucky, but I have my own all-but daunting tales and have heard hundreds more from sane and sober victims.

What are not so famous are the pitfalls of any small degree of success. Here I don't speak of the genuine rewards of sympathetic response—the sustaining letters from friends and strangers, the rare near-total comprehension. I mean the temptations offered by the sizable academic industry that has risen in the past thirty years round university study of contemporary letters—reading circuits, college residencies, community arts programs. God bless them, of course—large numbers of writers, especially poets, support themselves on such troubadour rounds. But at an invariably high cost to their own central task, the prose or verse. Anyone can name the famous figures, whirling the map like Dante's Lost, revenants of their former selves—exhausted but spieling for tidy sums. Omit names of the living; think only, for warning, of Auden in his last tragic decade. Not that his muffled isolation, his air of slow dissolution, was caused by the annual months on the road; but surely the road—indispensable to his financial survival—contributed hugely to the misery. His late poem, "On the Circuit," is a ruefully hilarious capture of the dilemma—

I shift so frequently, so fast,
I cannot now say where I was
The evening before last. . . .

Seldom discussed also are the internecine wars of rivalry and reputation—the jockeying for grants, prizes, and jobs (though these particular wars seem more endemic among poets than novelists, a result probably of the comparatively direr state of poetry as a popular form but also of the characteristic psychic composition of poets as distinct from novelists).

How much of that is autobiographical bellyaching, applicable to me but to few others? Virtually none—I'd wager that there aren't ten serious writers in America who wouldn't subscribe to a similar bill of grievances. Are the grievances special to the class then, to writers as opposed to academics or stereo salesmen or network vice-presidents? My guess is, yes. The business of writing is unavoidably a cottage industry, a one-man band; it can be well or poorly performed according to the competence and will of the writer. The business of publishing is not remarkably unlike many other medium-sized American industries. It could be well-organized and humanely and attentively conducted, to the mutual profit of producer (the writer), middle-man (the publisher), and consumer (the reader). It almost invariably is not so organized or conducted. Indeed, the last really fruitful innovation in American publishing was the revival, in the 1940s, of a nineteenth-century staple—the inexpensive paperbound book. Maybe we should farm the whole business out to Japanese sub-contractors. A touchingly small amount of clever attention would issue in startling results, I'm sure. If you still doubt me, ask to see the liquor (or comparable drug) bills of any five *successful* writers.

So stop, as I urged some pages back.

You almost certainly won't. Then I must tell you what I've withheld till now—the reasons for continuing. The first is persistent compulsion, though not necessarily obsession (the majority of bad writers are gravely obsessed). You are compelled—by the pressure of your entire life to this moment, by the pressure of a need to reward your loved ones, to reward yourself, and to thank the Powers—to sit in your room alone and form comely orderly tangible objects in ink on paper. If you sense further that the source of your compulsion is transcendent—God or a god—both your strength and your difficulties will be greater. A compulsion derived from the love of other human beings, in the hope of serving them and securing their devotion, will be constantly endangered by the very quality which you love in them—their beautiful solubility in time. Whatever your sense of the source, you cannot know from one day to the next that it will endure; there are no visible gauges to measure the fuel. You will need great lashings of reckless faith. You have some now; you must ration it sanely and replenish as you can. You should also nurse a notion of how to proceed should faith or compulsion itself expire. My own notion leans on the comforting prospect of manual work—drafting or some job of joinery that requires whole days of patient mindless sanding (no one who hasn't done a long stint of writing knows the degree to which it's *manual* labor, but do carpenters dream all night of their joints?).

The other reasons for continuing are surprisingly subsumed under the name *pleasure.* The tradition for thinking of writing as one of the grander agonies of the race is so ancient and so assiduously maintained by contemporary writers and critics that the idea of writing as pleasure is likely to seem coarse, to smack of the atmosphere of summer workshops in the Finger Lakes (much cuddling in the conifers)—poetry as Fulfillment, as Revenge, as Spiritual Calisthenic.

Unfortunately, the more enduring pleasures do not submit to discussion. They are experienced in the deep interior, in still isolation, and are no more communicable or desirous of communication than other mystic recompense. By a comparison with saints, I do not mean to imply that writers in their moments of rare satisfaction have exceeded other mortals. Again I suspect that craftsmen of the readily palpable—tables, houses, gardens—experience similar reward. Maybe the nearest hit would be this—the writer, successful in his own terms, knows the satisfaction of the parent of a perfect child: and a child who remains perfect long after the parent has ceased to care or to exist.

It is worth warning that the rewards seem to have no relation to external achievement or success. Many of the most "rewarded" of writers are famously miserable; the virtual hermits (Dickinson, Kafka, G. B. Edwards) appear to have known numerous exaltations. Without, again, barging farther into autobiography than would be useful here, I can add my own testimony—as a man who was reared in two large families whose only "creators" were fertile women, I think I can say that I've experienced more, and more continuous, reward from my writing than the big majority of workers I've known—whatever the work. I would hate to lose the impulse, though I trust it wouldn't kill me.

More ephemeral but real pleasures are concomitant—invitations to travel, chances to meet other writers who (whatever their normal neuroses) often make excellent short-term company, possible brief freshets of money, and an odd priestly status which the trade itself awards one. Interesting people who are not themselves writers (and alas, leaden bores as well) will yield you their total secrets at the flash of your writer's badge. You will be a sort of renegade confessor from here on and must view the office, with large grains of salt, as sacramental and of grave responsibility. You must also quickly develop techniques for stemming the flood of talk, with its vampire demands on sympathy and concentrated energy; you will need a battery of ways to say No, Oriental in delicacy and German in firmness.

With that, I've told you two-thirds of what I know after twenty-six years of steady writing—fiction, verse, drama, criticism, journalism. Since I plainly haven't deterred you in your own intention, though my initial Stop-sign wasn't displayed flippantly, I can close by speaking of the final and most important third, the way to proceed. Or ways—there are millions but all share certain inevitable traits.

The foundation of all else is the recognition that serious work commences in the unconscious mind, or is first received there, and is transmitted in quantities and at rates always in control of the unconscious faculties. The prime skill and discipline, therefore, is learning how to serve and thus partly master that source and governor. The discipline, as usual, divides into spiritual and physical departments.

The unconscious mind apparently resides in a physical organ, the brain. The brain has needs as urgent and as comprehensible as those of, say, the liver. You must learn the peculiar needs of your brain—how much sleep, how much sobriety; how much company, sex, drugs, fresh air. You must learn the rate of its movement—its *optimum* rate, the speed at which it will generate your work when you have dealt with it in intelligent respect. Such understanding is available only after a series of experiments upon oneself—how much of this or that can I take? Do I work most fruitfully in the morning or at night? How much must I produce in a day? (if I'm a novelist anyhow—one of the built-in blessings of fiction writing is its ready submission to diurnality; with the abandonment of long narrative, the contemporary poet is faced with a spasmodic and considerably more unnerving situation). But the understanding is as urgent and indispensable as the compulsion, the gift itself. Without it, you may give off a few smoky flares of reckless brevity; but a useful long-paced incandescence will elude you. If you answer that you positively desire brief flaring, then treat yourself to a careful study of the final letters of Rimbaud—not the brilliant nasty-boy letters but the achingly lonely groans from Africa.

The spiritual department must be your own look-out—yours and whatever masters you can find; even I won't venture to accompany you thence. I do know, however, that constant attention to physical and chronological discipline is among the strong tonics for all other healths.

To end then—it's a hard life. At least as hard as being a good parent and likely to last longer than parenting, harder than all the jobs which permit themselves to be switched off at the end of eight hours; maybe a little easier than being a good doctor or nurse, an earnest religious. But such gauging is absurd, in your case. You are not out for ease. You're out, I trust, for goodness—the perfection of your own peculiar compulsion, as a means of serving, maybe even augmenting the huge and permanent beauty of the visible world? the unseen piers on which the world rides.

Be good,
R. P.

Megan Staffel

Megan Staffel has published three works of fiction—the novels *She Wanted Something Else* and *The Notebook of Lost Things* and the collection *A Length of Wire and Other Stories.* She lives in New York State with her husband and children and teaches in the Adult Degree Program at Vermont College. "Laurie" was one of her students in that program.

A lesson, here, in how to use the uncertainty that accompanies getting started.

Dear Laurie

Dear Laurie:

I'm sorry you're having trouble getting started on a story about your father, but that's exactly what should be happening. The mistake people make when they think about writing has to do with the assumption of ease. In other words, because you can write, you assume that you can write fiction. But writing fiction requires the same kind of struggles that doing anything new requires. You wouldn't expect someone to be able to waterski without falling down on their first try; well, it's the same thing with fiction. The only difference is that it will continue to be a struggle even after you've done a lot of fiction writing. It's just the nature of the process. I think that the struggle comes from the situation. That is, every time you sit down to write you face yourself—your memories, your fears, your desires. And in your case, you're facing your father too. So along with the normal difficulties that everyone has when writing fiction, you're also facing whatever issues there are between yourself and your father. That's probably why you chose to write about him, there was something you needed to find out. So trust that. Stick with your choice. But trick yourself a little. This is easy to do. We're all very gullible. Fictionalize your father. If he has lots of hair, make him bald. If he never laughs, make him laugh a lot, etc. Make him appear to be someone different. You'll still get to what you need to get to, you'll still find the story, but it may be a little easier with your father in a costume. The other thing that you have to trust is the process. The story will come. And a story can be lots of things, it can be anything from forty words to four hundred pages. Let the story come. Don't edit yourself. You have to write some crap first. Sounds like exactly what you're doing. And then you have to put the crap in an envelope and send it to me. Remember when we went over that? This is the first step. Think about how a baby starts talking. They make some sounds first. Then they find their way to sentences, then to paragraphs, and then at five years old, bang! they don't shut up! You have to make some sounds first. Any sounds. Any sounds and then sentences, paragraphs, pages will come. I'm going to love whatever it is that you send me because I love fiction. So I'm very easy to work with. Also, I assume that everything you write is made up. So you can tell me unbelievable and horrific things about yourself and I will assume that you've made them up. And remember this is unlike anything else that you've ever done because you start from the point of not-knowing. You have to start there. Nowhere else in life are you ever told that. We're always supposed to know things. But here, in this process, you start with what you don't know, just like a baby making its first sounds. The writing will start to take shape eventually, but in the first draft you don't need to give that any thought. Your only job right now is to make those sounds.

Have fun—

Megan

Melanie Rae Thon

Melanie Rae Thon's most recent book is the collection of stories *First, Body.* She is also the author of two novels, *Meteors in August* and *Iona Moon,* and the story collection *Girls in the Grass.* Her fiction has been included in *The Best American Short Stories* (1995 and 1996), and she has received grants from the National Endowment for the Arts, the Massachusetts Artists Foundation, the New York Foundation for the Arts, and the Mrs. Giles Whiting Foundation. In 1996, the literary journal *Granta* included Thon on its list of twenty "Best Young American Novelists." Originally from Montana, she now teaches at the Ohio State University.

How to find yourself as a writer by losing yourself and all that you thought you knew about writing.

Letter to a Young Fiction Writer

My friend—

I forget how to write.

Every story presents its own problems. For twenty-two years I've done this work, but I'm a beginner every time, searching for a new voice and a path that will lead to territory I haven't charted.

I need mystery. I start with questions: *Why would a man try to lift a 326-pound corpse so gently? Did the slave murder her master's son; and if she did, why does the slave owner's daughter feel guilty?* There's no reason to follow a story if I know where I'm going. It's the process of discovery, the journey itself, that exhilarates me.

Working on my second novel, *Iona Moon,* destroyed my ability to craft short fiction. Now I do endless explorations and revisions. Later, I chisel, hoping to find a few true scenes or a spark of revelation. For "Little White Sister," a twenty-page piece, I wrote more than two hundred pages, the history of a man's memories and experiences: his attempt to slaughter a bull, his baptism, a field where two cousins seduced him. I did another fifty pages in the voice of a woman who speaks only seventeen lines. But when I composed her final monologue, I knew exactly what she had to say, and what was behind it.

I've made nine other stories since then, and for each one I've written enough pages and done enough research to fill a novel. It's not efficient, not economically expedient. But I write to understand my people, and I don't know any other way to do this. Some writers I admire are able to *think* their stories first, type them, tinker, and be finished. Once, thirteen years ago, a story came that way to me. Gift or trick, I thought at last I'd learned how to make fiction. Never again have I been so lucky. I need the movement of my hand, the flow of ink, months or sometimes years of contemplation. Hours of work give me rare moments of insight: I see an image I hadn't expected to find; I hear the right phrase with which to render it.

Most days, I'm slow and stupid. I have to read everything aloud, over and over—I'm speaking now as I write—because for me, sense comes from the sounds of words as much as from their definitions.

When I tried to uncover "Little White Sister," I tormented myself even more than usual. The critic in my head would not stay silent. I ranted. This was not my story. I was too ignorant and had no right to tell it. How could a white woman from Montana presume to speak in the voice of a black man from Boston? But Jimmy Diggs haunted me: I walked his streets; I tried to picture the swirling snow and scared woman he'd seen from his apartment window.

As I investigate any story, I ask myself: *Do I respect my people? Are their lives becoming real to me?*

Actor and playwright Anna Deavere Smith says that our failure to empathize may come from an inhibition, or reluctance to see. In her play *Fires in the Mirror,* she performs every role, transforming herself from Jewish woman to black activist, from the grieving father of a dead Guyanan child to the raging brother of a Hasidic scholar. She says that given enough time, everyone will say something that is like poetry. She tries to reiterate each person's pursuit of that poetic moment. By imitating another's words and rhythms, she recreates the cooperative dance of body and language. The act of speech, she says, is a physical act, and the search for character is in constant motion. "The spirit of acting is the *travel* from the self to the other."[1]

I believe this is also the spirit of writing fiction. Anna Deavere Smith's performance gave me the permission I needed to finish "Little White Sister." I no longer worried about breaking taboos. I no longer cared who might judge me.

My job was to pay attention to details. To listen. Jimmy Diggs was a drummer. He taught me to hear music as he did. The beat beneath melody and lyrics took on new meaning. Through this small opening of the senses, this altered perception, I finally glimpsed someone else's story. Insects buzzed in the woods, a sound beneath all other sounds. I heard the pulse under the words of his parents' arguments.

It took me six weeks to get it down. The last week, I worked obsessively, in eighteen-hour stretches. I couldn't sleep. I chanted. Every memory had a rhythm. When I spoke in it, the man's frenzy filled me. His remorse and anger emerged through language and became a purely physical sensation.

I remind myself of this often. It is not the "success" or "failure" of the work that gives it value. It is only the way it changes you, the way you begin to perceive the invisible, those events and passions beyond your own experience.

This is why I write. This is why it scares me.

Norman Maclean is one who has given me faith in the importance of the process. When he was seventy-four, he started exploring the story of fifteen Smokejumpers. Twelve of these men lost their lives fighting the Mann Gulch forest

---

[1] Anna Deavere Smith's comments on her work come from the introduction to *Fires in the Mirror* (1993), published by Anchor Books.

fire. At eighty-seven, Norman Maclean died, leaving the project publishable but unfinished. In *Young Men and Fire,* he says: "Unless we are willing to escape into sentimentality or fantasy, often the best we can do with catastrophes, even our own, is to find out exactly what happened and restore some of the missing parts."[2]

The task he set for himself was both impossible and humble; the important thing was to try to do it. In our desire to understand, in the constant movement between ourselves and others, we may find redemption.

[2]*Young Men and Fire* (1992), by Norman Maclean, is published by the University of Chicago Press.

John Updike

John Updike has been one of America's most distinguished writers of prose fiction (as well as a highly regarded essayist and poet) since his publication, in 1959, of *The Poorhouse Fair.* His work abounds with superb, evocative description, and his sensual imagery is noteworthy. Updike has chronicled the sexual and religious yearnings of the American middle class in his novels about Rabbit Angstrom—*Rabbit Run, Rabbit Redux, Rabbit Is Rich*—and his short stories about the Maples. Among his esteemed books are *The Centaur, Couples, The Witches of Eastwick, Pigeon Feathers, Bech: a Book,* and the literary essays in *Hugging the Shore* and *Odd Jobs.* He has been awarded the Pulitzer Prize and numerous other honors.

For one summer, Updike taught fiction writing at Harvard; in that class, he remembers two students who became working writers; one, Nicholas Delbanco, here receives praise for and instruction on the first two chapters of what would be his first novel, The Martlet's Tale.

Two Communications to
Nicholas Delbanco, Summer 1962

Well, this makes me feel fairly worthless as a writing instructor, but I have very few suggestions for improvement, at least allowing for this being the start of a novel, with no need to tie up all the threads here and with a certain generality in scene-laying allowed. For a beginner, you seem remarkably knowing in the trade of the novelist. This has size and speed both—some of the dialogue is quite wonderful and the prose is steadier, more consistently controlled and alive, than any I have looked at so far. At moments it reads a touch too much like a tourist's Greece described; but by and large you get into this landscape very well—uncannily well. In revising, you might want to watch your opening sections for a certain diffuseness—the ride in the ambulance perhaps is too chopped up, with explanations and small flashbacks—and what you have so far are not so much characters as promises of characters, but promising promises they are, and I hope you will go ahead now buoyed up by the excellence of what you have done.

. . .

In many ways this is better than the previous section, and I congratulate you. The language, as you can see from the sparsity of my comments, by and large resists criticism. . . . About the lovemaking itself . . . I have reservations, reservations not so much concerned with the propriety of close description as with the quality of this particular description. You almost do convey the, as it were, personality of this copulation, but the language too closely verges on the hysterical and the emptily ecstatic. It is foolish to deny that such a passage arouses a certain extra-aesthetic pornographic interest, and as such deserves extra care. I think you could do it better. My chief reservation, on the 68 pages I have read, is that you hint at, rather than achieve, characterization. Sotiris remains—as you once said—an empty center. Dania (except for the stammer and the vivid glimpse of her heart on pp. 64–5) is rather vague, and even Mehmet Effendi is not so much a person as a piece of human furniture. At no point do you give the dialogue its head; but seem always to be editing as we go. This is, I think, because as yet Sotiris does not really engage your interest. When your interest *is* engaged, i.e., in the sounds and smells of your city, you write admirably. But until these details become the envelope of a clear and legible emotion, ambition, or dilemma, the reader's interest, while respectful, will be to some extent merely polite. I think your stiffness will tend to work itself out as your imagination, more secure in its setting, exercises itself in the momentum of a plot. Good luck.

James Welch

James Welch was born in Browning, Montana, in 1940. He is an enrolled member of the Blackfeet Tribe, and attended schools on the Blackfeet and Fort Belknap Reservations, graduating from high school in Minneapolis, Minnesota, in 1958. He received a B.A. from the University of Montana in 1965 and spent two years in the M.F.A. Program in Creative Writing at the University of Montana, studying with poet Richard Hugo. He has written a book of poems (*Riding the Earthboy 40*) and four novels (*Winter in the Blood, The Death of Jim Loney, Fools Crow,* and *The Indian Lawyer*). His most recent work, nonfiction, is *Killing Custer.* He has taught at the University of Washington and Cornell University. Welch has received many awards, including the Los Angeles Times Book Prize for fiction, an American Book Award, a Chevalier de L'Ordre des Arts et des Lettres from France, and honorary doctorates from Rocky Mountain College and the University of Montana. He is currently working on a novel about a Lakota Indian who went to France with Buffalo Bill's Wild West Show in 1889.

To a Native American who wishes to write, from a Native American who is one of this country's most distinguished writers.

Letter to a Young Writer

Dear Robert,

In response to the letter you sent a couple of weeks ago, I send you a big, fat YES. If you've got the imagination, the talent and the perseverence, if you have stories to tell, and if you possess strong medicine and a little luck, you can be a writer.

You state in your letter that you are an enrolled member of the Crow tribe but you haven't lived on the reservation since you were twelve years old. Just to complicate things, you are a mixed-blood, having an Irish grandfather on your mother's side and a Frenchman way back there on your father's side. Welcome to the club, Robert—ninety-eight percent of Indian writers are either mixed-bloods or half-breeds.

You didn't say how you got to Seattle and the University of Washington, only that you are a junior majoring in English with an American Indian Studies minor. And last quarter you took a fiction-writing class "as a lark," which you now feel may have changed your life forever. And now you would like to pursue this newfound love for language and storytelling.

First, let me say you have taken the correct first step toward a writing career (but it's a teeny tiny step). Virtually all of the Indian writers I know, or know of, started their careers with at least one writing course in college. Which assumes quite correctly that virtually all Indian writers went to college. So you're on track, Robert.

I should point out that there are a lot of writers who deride the idea of college writing courses. These are usually older writers, who may have begun their careers as old-fashioned journalists, writing hard every day, interviewing disagreeable but important people, meeting deadlines, arguing with editors—you name it. They feel they have done it the hard way, they have earned what success they enjoy, and everybody should have to put in such a rigorous apprenticeship. The common refrain here, when speaking of the young writers who go through writing programs, is this: "Writing can't be taught. Either you've got it or you don't. And you get it by getting out there and facing the world head-on." The implication is that writing programs coddle young would-be writers into thinking they have the real goods when in reality they're young pups who haven't experienced anything; therefore, they have nothing to write about, nothing to say.

Do you have nothing to say, Robert? Nothing to write about? I assume that you are probably twenty, twenty-one. That's awfully young to be considering a career in writing. When I was your age, I had already failed out of two colleges and was going nowhere. It was a scary time. I was working as a seasonal employee for the Forest Service down in California and thinking that this was going to be my life. I knew a few men in their thirties or forties who were doing exactly that—working from April to November, building fire lines, repairing trails, fighting fire, repainting buildings and repairing tools for the next season. Of course, the young college kids looked up to them—they were experienced, some of them were crew bosses, most of them were squad bosses on fires. During the summer season, I suspect that these seasonal "lifers" enjoyed this status—but I often wondered what they thought about their lives during the off-season. Was it a time for introspection, for spiritual renewal—or was it a time of those small terror attacks that come at odd times, such as when one is popping a beer, or checking the mail (nothing), or opening the door of the car and realizing that you have nowhere to go? Nowhere to go, Robert—maybe that's the definition of a life wasted. And after failing out of two schools and working as a seasonal employee for what could have been the rest of my life, I was on the verge of fulfilling that definition.

What does the above story have to do with anything? What does it have to do with you? You seem to have your stuff together—you mention that you went to college right after high school and that you are doing well as a student. It seems you are in no danger of becoming what I almost became. Maybe the point of the story is that I had a significant (awful) life experience at your age, and while I didn't write about it per se, the main characters in my first two novels live a kind of seasonal life, filled with small terror attacks, with really no place to go. So, you see, stories can come from anywhere, at any age, in any form—sometimes the experience can become a straight line into the heart of the story; other times, it can be transformed into a completely different situation, but often that significant experience will only set the mood or tone of a narrative far removed from the actual experience.

I should tell you one other thing about that period in my life—I was writing. I started writing in high school, probably when I was a junior. I wrote poems in study hall; I wrote poems in the evening when I should have been doing homework. Later, when I was working for the Forest Service, I would sprawl under a Ponderosa or a Sugar pine, fill my nostrils with that sweet, ashy odor of a hot California forest, and write. Sometimes the writing came in the form of a poem; other times, it turned out to be a small vignette about a guy lying under a pine tree, with a hornet buzzing around his nose and buzzards circling in the blue sky above him. Sometimes I would stretch my imagination and write about the seashore with its crashing waves and wheeling gulls.

I was full of clichés in those days, Robert. I had a set of clichés for any situation you can imagine. If I wrote about the lovely, unattainable cheerleaders, they were always blonde and pert and prancing. In my seashore poems, the gulls were always wheeling. If I set my vignette in a forest setting, the trees were stately, the mountains unfailingly majestic.

I know I'm digressing, Robert, but just let me ramble on for another minute, then we'll get back to whatever advice I can offer you. Or maybe I'm giving you something to think about, just doing it in a more narrative form. And I should warn you that, since I began my writing career as a poet, much of what I will tell you about this writer's beginnings revolves around poetry.

During those fairly miserable early years of college, I kept notebooks—those half-size spiral notebooks with the shiny brown covers. I filled them up with words—mostly poems, but a few vignettes, a few snatches of wisdom, a moment or two of intense beauty. Oh, and here's another thing, Robert: I was always embarrassed, even half-ashamed, of my literary efforts. I never showed my work to anyone. You see, back in those days—the late fifties, very early sixties—a real man didn't write poems. That was for sissies and fairies. A real man, say between the ages of sixteen and twenty-two, played sports or worked on cars. He was obsessed with screwing girls. And when, on those fairly rare occasions he was successful, he told his buddies, and they all looked at the victim with a keen hunger in their eyes. Will I be next in line?

But I was intensely shy. I don't think I had a date in high school or my first couple of years in college. In class I talked only when called upon. Once in a while I would take a wild guess at the answer, but more often, I would simply say, "I don't know." It was easier to be dumb than have a teacher try to "draw me out," which more than one attempted. Happily, or unhappily, they would eventually give up on me.

Are you getting the impression that I was a "loser" back in those days, Robert? I thought so too—my parents, teachers, everybody thought so—but I wasn't. It turns out I was doing exactly the right things a would-be writer should do. I was working in my notebooks—copying poems and stories that I liked in longhand, imitating them, then writing my own original compositions. Actually the imitations were the most fun. If I read "Because I Could Not Stop for Death," I would then write my own version. I still remember a lot of the poems I imitated: "Stopping by Woods on a Snowy Evening," "Mister Flood's Party," "In a Station of the Metro." One of my favorites was "Portrait," by E. E. Cummings ("Buffalo Bill's defunct . . ."), but the one that inspired me to great heights as imitator was "Paradise Lost." I wrote twelve pages of fast and furious verse—it was like I had sprung a leak and the words were careening around the room like a passel of farting balloons. All I had to do was chase them down.

You may wonder how a young man, who was in the process of failing out of Northern Montana College, came to be familiar with great poetry. Two books, Robert: ONE HUNDRED AND ONE FAMOUS POEMS and UNDERSTANDING POETRY. I bought the FAMOUS POEMS for a dollar in 1960 and I still have it. It's the first book of poems I'd ever owned. I'm embarrassed to admit it, but my name is written in gold ink across the top of the cover—James P. Welch, Jr.—in gold! Perhaps appropriately, some of the "famous poems" were quite bad, but I didn't know that. To me, Edgar A. Guest was every bit as wondrous as William Wordsworth; John Greenleaf Whittier as musical as Emily Dickinson or Lord Byron. I just didn't have a clue back in those days, Robert. But then I took an English course and the text was UNDERSTANDING POETRY, an anthology/textbook edited by Cleanth

Brooks and Robert Penn Warren, which I still have and which may have been the single most valuable book in my college career. Of course, I was too dumb to realize this at the time, but I loved that book. It covered all the bases of poetry, from metrics to imagery to theme to metaphor to form.

Unfortunately, the book was not of much use when it came time to take a poetry-writing course. A couple of years later, I enrolled at the University of Montana, and a year after that, I took my first poetry workshop (see, we've come full circle, Robert—back to writing classes, and now I'll try to tell you what I found valuable about them—but at my own pace and in my own way).

My poetry teacher was a youngish middle-aged man by the name of Richard Hugo. Maybe you've heard of him? He was born and raised in Seattle, or more properly, White Center, a working class section of Seattle. He later went to the University of Washington, then enlisted in the Army Air Corps, became a bombardier, and flew way too many missions during World War II. After the war he went back to school and studied poetry with Theodore Roethke. Then he worked for Boeing as a tech writer for fourteen years. So when he came to the University as an assistant professor, he had already lived quite a life. But this was his first teaching job and he was as frightened as a lamb in a shitstorm of coyotes.

As a kid, he fished the Duwamish River and a small creek that ran through White Center. He played baseball, and later, softball. He eventually became good enough to play in one of the top softball leagues in Seattle. For the rest of his life, he was obsessed with fishing, and fish, and softball. That obsession with things at a young age later translated into an obsession with poetry and language, and yes, things, which I think all great poets possess. This is a bit of a double entendre,

Robert. All great poets must possess their worlds and the things that are in it. So for instance, when Hugo came to Montana for his first teaching job, he looked at an abandoned ranch and he possessed it: This is my ranch and now I will tell you the tragic story of the family that once lived here but is now long gone. The poem, "Montana Ranch Abandoned," would break your heart, Robert. He got it exactly right, although I don't think he knew the difference between a corral and a chicken coop.

The first class I took from Hugo made me realize that I didn't know anything about contemporary poetry, or as I called it back in those days, "modern" poetry. All that stuff about meter and symbol and theme didn't do me a bit of good. All of the "great" poems I copied into my notebooks were irrelevant. Hugo would talk about rhythm and images and voice and emotion and psychology. He would encourage us to use internal rhymes and half-rhymes for the sake of the rhythm, never end-rhymes—okay, maybe once in a while, when the poem demanded it. Robert, I lived and died on end-rhymes. That was the fun of poetry, to make the words at the ends of lines rhyme, no matter how torturously. I was good at it, Robert, good, I tell you.

And symbols! I had a million symbols in me and now Hugo was telling me to forget them! But what about The Tree of Life, The Misbegotten Moon, The Lost Geese? Forget them—a tree is a tree, the moon the moon, the geese geese. They'll find their own identity. You just concentrate on the language, the images, the rhythm, the words, the syllables. If the moon enters your poem, it will be what it is, and then, more. Don't worry about it.

Needless to say, Robert, that class was a bit discouraging. I felt like I had homeschooled myself and ordered the wrong books from the wrong company. This "modern" poetry was nothing like my beloved Henry Wadsworth Longfellow's "By the shores of Gitche Gumee. . . ." But I wrote poems for the workshop—thin little poems that rarely lasted more than ten lines; lifeless little poems that were as hollow as empty toilet paper tubes. For some reason Hugo was gentle with me. He would jump on one of the more experienced poets with both feet when they screwed up ("What the hell happened here?"). They should know better. But he knew right away that I didn't know better. So he would very tactfully tear my poem apart, then roar with delight over the one little thing I did right—"Jesus Christ, that three-legged dog swimming in a bowl of tapioca is just great!"

I think I wrote five poems in that class, each one less ebullient than the last. At the end of the quarter I figured I wasn't much of a poet, that I'd better try to get my old job with the Forest Service back. Let me repeat—I was discouraged, Robert. Seemed I wasn't cut out to be a poet, after all.

But a funny thing happened about a month later. I wrote a poem that really looked like a poem. It almost seemed like I knew what I was doing. Then I wrote another the next day. And another. For the next year and a half I was writing five or six poems a week. I don't know what happened. Maybe, to use one of Hugo's favorite phrases, "the sucker lights came on." I began to understand what a poem was, what it could do, what I could do in it. In any case, I became obsessed with writing poems. Even when I was just walking home from the grocery store (which was rare—I was the working definition of the starving poet), or drinking beer at the local watering hole, I was thinking of words. I could look at an old man crossing the street, and the first line of a poem would come into my head.

I won't kid you, Robert—most of those poems were pretty dreary. But I was trying different things—different stanza lengths, different line lengths, writing in different voices. I was trying various ways to vary the rhythm. And perversely, I was trying to figure out ways to end-rhyme so that a reader might hear a familiarity of sound without knowing where it came from. Finally, after a year and a half, I had about five poems that I thought were pretty good, so I sent them out. I won't bore you with my rejection slip stories, buddy. You'll find out all about them if you decide that you really want to put in the work to become a writer. I will tell you this—rejection of your work is never easy to take. You put so much of yourself in your poems or stories or whatever that it feels like the faceless editor, or more likely, an assistant editor, is rejecting not just your work but you. They're pretty much saying that you are not a worthwhile human being, that you should go back to your cave and eat raw meat or—in my case— whatever you do out there in Montana.

Well. You must be thinking at this point, What's going on here—I ask for a little advice and the guy ends up telling me his life story. Who's this about, me or him? Well, bear with me a little longer. I might be able to give you a little advice, maybe not. First, I have to tell you how those floodgates opened and the poems came pouring out. Toward the end of that writing class, maybe after my fourth or fifth poem, Hugo was strangely silent. The other student-poets were very dutifully suggesting what went wrong and how I could fix it. I very dutifully, if faint-heartedly, listened and took notes. Finally, we had exhausted all the possibilities and we looked to Hugo for his comments. He liked to let the students battle back and forth, then he would make his pronouncements. This time, he kept his head down for a few dramatic beats while we waited; then he looked up at me and said, "What do you really know about?" You have to remember, Robert—I was painfully shy and self-effacing in those days and seldom spoke. I felt all my classmates' eyes boring into my very soul. I was as naked as a jaybird at that moment. I think I mumbled, "Not much, I guess." "But you must have come from someplace, you must know something." I think I just looked at him. "Where are you from?" I could at least answer that: "I was born on the Blackfeet Reservation, my father's reservation, lived there for a while, and eventually moved down to the Fort Belknap Reservation, my mother's reservation, where my father tried ranching with my grandfather." Hugo brightened: "I *thought* you were an Indian. Why don't you write about being an Indian? Write about that landscape out there, the people in it."

This was back in the sixties, Robert. Many things were going on in this country—the Viet Nam war, the peaceniks. Both Kennedys and Martin Luther King had been assassinated. It was an amazing time of change, of hostility, of great energy and great loss. Who in the world would want to read poems about Indians on reservations in northern Montana? Indians were the forgotten people in America. It wouldn't be until the early seventies, until the occupation of Alcatraz and some federal buildings, and the standoff at Wounded Knee, that Indians would enter the consciousness of this country. Unfortunately, they left the consciousness as quickly as they entered.

But let's not get into politics, Robert. That's a whole other subject, although, as you might guess, virtually all Indian writing is political in one way or another. The trick is to get your message across by showing, not telling. Hugo used to say if you've got a message, send a telegram. I know what his message was in that statement, but I don't totally agree with it. My method has always been to disguise the message through story. But very definitely send a message. Wake them up in the middle of the night but don't grab them by the throat. I think that's why the American Indian Movement fizzled out after Wounded Knee. Americans just grew weary of being seized by the throat. They grew weary of collective guilt. Even those who were sympathetic with the movement began to feel used and abused. But the Indian writers continue to shake Americans awake with their more measured yet persistent delivery. That's the power of good writing.

Where were we, Robert? Oh yes, I was saying that I didn't think Hugo's suggestion about writing about Indians in northern Montana was a very good one, that nobody would be interested. I was wrong. That's all I can say about that. I've made a decent living by writing about Indians. In my novels, I've tried to write about different Indian people in different situations—from derelicts on the reservation to a lawyer on the rise in a political setting. I even wrote a historical novel because I wanted to show what life was like for Indians just before the white man subdued them. My purpose? To show that Indians had a civilization, that they were human beings, that they lived in a fine-tuned accordance with the temporal and spiritual world. They weren't savages in the derogatory sense of that word.

All this is to say that you can do anything you want, say anything you want, tell any story that you like, use any language that strikes you. You can even send a message, if you do it well.

I know you are interested in fiction, in writing stories, and eventually, novels. And here I've gone on about poetry. I should feel guilty, Robert, but I don't. To paraphrase one of my favorite writers, Elio Vittorini, all writings come out of a single bottle.

What advice can I give you? I honestly don't know. I can say the usual things—keep your ass nailed to the chair until something comes; don't worry about copywriting your deathless prose; keep your dobber up in the face of countless rejections; accept success gracefully; admit failure grudgingly; write smarter than you are; always make sure your editing pencil is sharp and ruthless.

And here's a piece of advice that a lot of young would-be writers find a little intimidating: Write steadily and hard for at least two years after you graduate. This is the lonely time. It's just you and your computer or typewriter or pencil and blank sheets of paper. Fill up those sheets. Try different things—different styles and techniques, different voices, weird dialogue, stream of consciousness—all those things you learned in class. Don't be afraid to experiment. Forget about finished pieces (and by that I mean pieces that you are writing for publication—eventually you will just naturally write some stories that sound right). Continue your newfound love affair with language. Become obsessed with words—with interesting verbs and adjectives. Avoid adverbs. If at the end of your two-year period, you feel good about your writing and your work habits, continue. If you have found your interest slacking; if you feel your writing is going nowhere; if you find that earning a living takes precedence over the writing—quit. No dishonor there. Enjoy the rest of your life.

Finally, Robert, I have not forgotten that you are an Indian and lived on the Crow Reservation for over half of your young life. I guess I haven't talked about your Indianness for a reason—it is up to you to decide if your ethnicity will become a large part of your identity, as well as the substance of your material. I suspect it will, but it is up to you. Just don't say "my people" a lot. That always sounds a bit disingenuous, especially if you haven't been around your people much and participated in the culture and traditions. But by all means write about them, if you choose.

So, there it is, Robert. I hope this ramble has helped some. Oddly enough it has helped me a great deal to remember those days when I was your age. It was such a thrill to write then. I envy you, buddy. Good luck.

Best wishes,
James Welch

Tobias Wolff

Tobias Wolff's books include the memoirs *This Boy's Life* and *In Pharaoh's Army;* the short novel *The Barracks Thief;* and three collections of stories: *In the Garden of the North American Martyrs, Back in the World,* and, most recently, *The Night in Question.* He teaches at Stanford University.

A memorable dressing-down to a writer who fails to respect his own talent; it is so accurate as to make every writer blush, and it is so generous as to suggest a round of applause.

To Jerry

2 Sept 79

Jerry:

I'm glad that Flannery O'Connor interests you, and that you've decided to make use of her work in your paper. It's a fantastic topic—really—and her stories will provide weight and balance to your studies of Southern and Friedman. And there's no question that you have a great deal to say on the subject of grotesques.

While we're on the subject of grotesques we might as well take a look at your stories (by the way, I thought *Slam* was going under; they broke their promise. What would it take, what would it cost me, to make sure that they *do* go under?). About *Watching Mom Die* the less said the better. The most amusing thing about it was of course your use of the word "Mom" which still has enough down-home sweetness, Ozzie-and-Harriet resonance so that using it in the context you created produced a small jolt every time it occurred. I confess I tittered here and there, though not often, and in every case what I found funny was either the word "Mom" or some other intrusion of the quotidian or wholesome into your madcap Mom-stuff. What's the lesson? Are we so jaded that the only thing left with power to amuse is "real life"? I s'peck so.

My Dad was much funnier, again largely because of a single word—"Dad." But the tone was funnier as well—"Dad was heck in traffic"—because in its aw-shucks All-American way it kept trying to contain the chaos which it narrated, rather than participating in the chaos, as the tone of most of your work does. Thus what you're really doing successfully is lampooning a tone. You do it very well, and the story is quite

249

funny. I'm sure someone will pick it up. Try *Iowa Review,* they go for things like this once in a while.

My reservation is this: what's the *point* of lampooning a tone that has so often been lampooned, sometimes (as in Lardner's *The Haircut*) with some purpose greater than the lampooning itself? You will say—*just for laughs. What's wrong with that?* Of course there's nothing *wrong* with that, but if it's enough for you then I think you're taking a dive, because you can do better. As for either *Mom* or *Dad* being "morally bankrupt," forget it. They don't have stature enough to be discussed in terms of their morality. Bladder bags, V.D., incest, racial jokes are not new. Riding the crest of some *nouvelle vague* is not exactly what you're doing, as I'm sure you know. The sorry truth is that after *National Lampoon* and *Zap* we've exhausted our capacity for surprise at these things. That's why the everyday stuff is so funny in your story. Hardly anything that is obviously calculated to shock will in fact produce that reaction any more. The reader knows all the moves.

There's no question that you're a born satirist. But the thing that good satire has that I find wanting in your work is some implied idea of the good of which the thing being satirized is an aberration or perversion. This touches, incidentally, on Flannery O'Connor's discussion of the grotesque in *Mystery and Manners.* In your letter you quote her as saying that "the reason Southern writers write about the grotesque so much is because they can still recognize it." If I'm not wrong she goes on to say that the reason they can still recognize the grotesque is because there is still in the South some common understanding of what comprises the Whole Man (her expression). In other words the distortion is emphasized not for its own sake but to point at some deficiency of which the distortion is a product.

Re-read Swift's *A Modest Proposal* and part iv of *Gulliver,* the sections dealing with the Yahoos. In *Proposal* Swift lampoons a tone, the rationalist-optimistic tone which is the signature of social theory in his time and ours, and he gets away with it because the horrors which he so cheerfully proposes are in fact preferable to the horrors which he hopes by his proposal to remedy. That's the cutting edge of the essay. And the humorous observations of the Yahoos are not simple misanthropy, but a way of talking about greed and cowardice and any number of other things. The Yahoos represent not only Swift's rather jaundiced view of humanity, but also Swift's disappointment in the particular hopes he had for humanity. From his idea of the good proceeded his idea of the grotesque; his idea of the good is the organizing principle of all his satire, and the source of it.

I'm not by habit a moralist, and you mustn't think that my habitual mode of address is the sermon. My idea of how to proceed with you ran something like this: here is a man who is a gifted satirist, a good writer, funny, unusual. He's losing his sting because he's not drawing his satire from any genuine anger about the way things are, or even despair. He needs to touch bottom again.

That's what I thought. That's why I gave you the reading list I gave you, not to make you into a better person but to make you into a better writer. I hoped that by thinking about these basic things again in a purposeful, deliberate way you could freshen whatever stores of outrage—or affirmation— you have. I still think that you can, but you do have to give the reading some respect, some thought, let it work on you. Did you really have no other reaction to "The Bible" as you call it—you didn't read the whole thing and I didn't ask you to— than that you were glad you didn't have to spend more time in motel rooms? If so I am wasting your time. It should at least, if it didn't convince you, have given rise to a sense of wonder, or outrage, or *something*. I don't care if you believe in Buddha or French Toast. I do want you to react to your reading, though, in a way that will help your writing. If my reading list is failing you here then let me know and we'll make up another. It just seems to me that you have a fair enough command of style and contemporary modes of writing that you ought to spend some time pondering the values that our literature has grown out of, and to make thoughtful rejections or adoptions as the spirit moves you. Sounds stiff but it's true. . . .

I thought you were going to be in New Mexico. Don't succumb to the lure of the bucks. Write some good fiction and I'll do my level best to help you get a fellowship somewhere. You're so fucking talented. Just cooperate, okay? Be a sport.

Yours ever,
Toby

Hilma Wolitzer

Hilma Wolitzer's novels include *Ending, Hearts,* and *Tunnel of Love.*
She's taught in several university writing programs and has held
Guggenheim and National Endowment for the Arts fellowships. She
received an Award in Literature from the American Academy and
Institute of Arts and Letters and the 1997 Barnes & Noble Writer for
Writers Award.

*The relationship of wage earning to the art of
fiction, and a reminder that a job will net you
more than the necessary paycheck.*

Supporting Your Habit

Dear Young Writer,

So *this* is what you've decided to do with your life. I'll bet your parents aren't exactly thrilled. When they were walking the floor with you during those long colicky nights, visions of a future neurosurgeon or international banker were probably what kept them going. But instead of supporting them grandly in their old age, you're off to work in your pajamas every day, at no one's behest, and without a guaranteed market for your product.

In a way, that's actually the *good* news. After all, there's no rush hour to contend with at home (except for the one inside your head), no boss on your back, and, if you ever do sell anything you've written, you can deduct a portion of your rent from your taxes. Writing is a solitary occupation, but not necessarily a lonely one; your characters can be a lot more fun than the crowd around the water cooler. As for your parents, they should remember that when they gave you life, they also gave you death, something they certainly weren't thinking about at the time. This chosen profession of yours may not undo their wanton bargain and make you immortal, but it does give you the chance to lead additional, imagined lives.

The bad news is pretty obvious: The rent on that (ultimately) tax-deductible space has to be paid, so if you aren't living with a non-writer, someone with an actual, paying job, you're going to have to support your writing habit by getting a job yourself. Of course these tidings disturb you. The time spent away from your *real* work may seem like a tragic waste and a serious distraction. The thing about writing is that it requires fierce, utter concentration and long, unbroken hours; this is a simple truth. We all know about Dickens' time lost to the blacking factory and Kafka's bitterness about having to labor as a clerk. And would-be writers who've stayed home to raise families might ruefully reflect on Virginia Woolf's words: "Often nothing tangible remains of a woman's day. The food that has been cooked is eaten, the children that have been nursed have gone out again into the world. What is the salient point for the novelist to seize upon?" What, indeed? And what are *you* trained to do, except enter the fictional dream?

Truthfully, I thought I'd beat the job rap. I do have a working husband, and early on it seemed as if I'd make a killing with my short stories. In 1965, when I was a young(ish) writer, myself, I sold the first one to a national magazine for the grand sum of $1250! I bought my first car that very afternoon—a white Rambler station wagon with a snazzy red interior and a roof rack. I was flooded by a sense of power. I figured if I could knock off a story a week, or even one a month, why, I'd probably end up with a *fleet* of Ramblers. It didn't quite work out that way. I was very prolific, but I didn't sell another story for three years, and this time it was to a small literary magazine for a small honorarium. Just enough for some gas for the Rambler. Despite my regularly employed husband, there came a time when I had to contribute more to our household income. That's when I began to teach writing, on a community, adult-ed level at first, and eventually in graduate schools. This is a common route for writers, and it's not without its irony—to earn a living teaching other people to do what you can't earn a living at yourself.

There's much more to regular employment, though, than just the money. Even works of the imagination depend on the distillation of real experience; Charlotte Brontë's post as a governess and Melville's short tenure on a whaler certainly informed their writing. But a more subtle fringe benefit of work may be on-the-job training in human psychology that's especially useful to fiction writers. It's safe to say that working contributed to Dickens' compassion for the underdog, and to Kafka's fear and loathing of authority. (Read "The Metamorphosis" for the best excuse ever for not getting to the office in the morning.) If fiction teaches one how to live, it's also conversely true that living teaches one how to write fiction. The major problem with some younger writers' novels about rootless, disaffected people is that these characters don't seem to have *earned* their estrangement, or our sympathy, any more than their green authors. Far worse than an unexamined life is one that's examined before it's been fully lived and absorbed. And what about life *outside* one's airless, interior self?

I love reading books about working people because they let me in on the otherwise unknowable life of the elusive "other." John Casey's novel *Spartina* tells me about boats and fishing, *Weeds* (a rediscovered novel written in 1923) by Edith Summers Kelley, offers the lowdown on scratch farming, and Philip Roth's *American Pastoral* includes a step-by-step explanation of glove manufacturing, all things I didn't even know interested me until I read about them. These books enrich my understanding of the exterior world, and become references for facts I might not easily have found elsewhere. Mary McCarthy wrote that the great novelists have in common "a deep love of fact," and I agree, but the most accurate and beautifully rendered facts by themselves don't make for good fiction. Only the facts as filtered through the lives of fully realized characters really resonate. That's why those well-researched, but curiously anemic blockbusters like James Michener's *Space,* about the development of that industry in the United States, don't linger very long in the mind, no matter how fascinating the subject may be. The truth is that *Weeds* isn't really about farming at all, but about *farmers,* both generic and particular people whose lives seem to evolve from the very soil they till, the soil in which, the reader comes to believe, they'll finally be laid to rest.

The problem with writing as an occupational source of material, is that it can be too solipsistic and too conscious of process and of language. It's not surprising that publishers are generally wary of novels whose fictional heroes are writers. Yet there are those who have taken this suspect experience and spun it into literary gold; Roth and John Irving come immediately to mind. Teaching writing has some of the same pitfalls as writing, itself, but Elizabeth Bishop managed to get a brilliantly sad and funny piece about her stint teaching a correspondence course at "The U.S.A. School of Writing." Although most of her students are remarkably untalented, more memorable for the mechanics of their writing than for its style or content—one woman decorates her homework with Christmas seals, and a man with a very large handwriting manages to inscribe only one sentence per page—Bishop still determines one day in the school's communal office that "it was here, in this noisome place, in spite of all I had read and been taught and thought I knew about it before, that the mysterious, awful power of writing first dawned on me." What she recognizes on the job, beside the pervasive authority of the printed word, is the striving of her desolate students toward an elusive communal happiness. For want of a better word, it's their *humanity* she sees, not a bad lesson for any writer to learn.

The resourceful novelist can get around the publishers' leeriness of writer-heroes by transposing the writing experience into allied artistic pursuits, like painting or photography or composing music. But there are solid reasons to stray even further afield. Primo Levi wrote of the ways his newer "trade" of writing plainly benefited from his former "trade" of chemistry. "The habit of penetrating matter, of wanting to know its composition and structure, foreseeing its properties and behavior, leads to an insight, a mental habit of concreteness and concision, the constant desire not to stop at the surface of things."

Good working habits, so to speak. Writers who have trouble just sitting down and shutting out the rest of the intrusive, seductive world, might benefit from the enforced discipline of a steady job. They might learn to keep established hours and get into the routine of meeting deadlines. As to Virginia Woolf's caveat to ambitious housewives, I can say from experience that domestic work, too, cultivates a kind of discipline useful to the writer. And there's pride taken in the most mundane work that parallels the pride taken in the fruits of the mind. Some feminists (and I consider myself one) might be troubled by this comparison, but the satisfaction of writing a story is eerily similar to that of completing some household chore, cleaning the hall closet, for instance. In either case, you're imposing temporary order onto chaos. Although I'd much rather write a story, and I haven't cleaned my closets in ages, I still remember the raw pleasure of finishing that dreaded job, and how I'd keep opening the closet door afterward, peeking inside for the renewable surprise of its organization, or to make some fussy, last-minute adjustment to a stray hanger or something on a shelf. How much like reading a just-written story—admiring it, certainly, but still critical, still making editorial changes.

Domesticity doesn't just impose good working habits, though. It also tenders insights into the dynamics of the family, that microcosm of the larger society, and it offers a wide range of images, from the brilliant, nervous beauty of a Jell-O mold to the steamy, starchy fragrance of laundry day. Every job or profession offers its own useful impressions. William Carlos Williams said that doctoring gave him entry "into the secret gardens of the self . . . a badge to follow the poor, defeated body into those gulfs and grottos." His famous short story "The Use of Force" beautifully bears him out. When the doctor in the story engages in a ferocious struggle with a child who won't let him examine her throat, he's finally rewarded with a view of the telltale membrane covering her tonsils. Now he can treat her diphtheria, but he's ashamed of the pleasure he takes in his victory, and mourns the loss of self his small patient has suffered in his invasion of her body.

Membrane, diphtheria. I can't help but note the oddly lyrical beauty of medical jargon, and the splendid opportunities it presents for metaphor. A doctor palpates for a "thrill" in a patient's pulse and for the "quickening" of an unborn fetus. And then there's the rippling alliteration of tetany, tendonitis, and torticollis. I'm not suggesting you drop everything and go off to medical school. Remember that carpenters may write with confidence of plumb bobs and caliper rules, and grill cooks and waiters have a coded language of their own.

I held some diverse jobs, myself, during the years before I began writing. I did assorted office work, including typing, filing, and operating a bookkeeping machine, and was, among other things, a feather fluffer and paster in a factory, a saleswoman, a babysitter, a renter of beach chairs under the boardwalk at Coney Island, a nursery school teacher, a junior social hostess at a Catskill Mountain resort, and, of course, a housewife. Looking back at all those jobs, and at my fiction, I see that, except for homemaking and typing, I haven't used much of that experience directly, but all of it has influenced my writing indirectly. For one, important thing, most of my characters are working-class people. I can genuinely empathize with the frustrations of a nine-to-five job and a limited (albeit steady) income.

Of course we can't be all things in this short life, and find time to write about them, too. For my own essentially non-technical novels, I've had to ask for help from experts in (among other fields) medicine, pharmacy, midwifery, jazz and classical music, sound engineering, and photography. The midwife I consulted for help with a childbirth scene in a novel told me that the mother's belly rises up in a point, like a witch's hat during the last stages of labor, and that the rupturing bag of waters has a strange, earthy smell—a little like summer rain—things I hadn't noticed during the deliveries of my own children (I guess I was too busy screaming), but that I pounced on to include in my novel. It's essential to get these things right; the willing suspension of disbelief we strive for from readers would be compromised by misinformation or mere techno-talk.

An argument might be made that we write (and read) in order to *escape* the reality that comes with our daily routines, with our jobs. But there are other more urgent reasons to read or write a book—to be educated, for instance, and to be consoled, and to connect ourselves to others on this vast and lonely planet.

I'd be lying, though, if I didn't say that I hope I never have to work at anything but writing (and maybe a little teaching) again as long as I live. And I wish you, after you've absorbed an appropriate amount of useful worldly experience, nothing but fat royalty checks and uninterrupted hours of dreaming and creating. But until then, I'd advise you to make the most of what you must do. Maybe Kipling says it best:

> "Seek your job with thankfulness and work till further orders,
> if it's only netting strawberries or killing slugs on borders;
> And when your back stops aching and your hands begin to harden,
> You will find yourself a partner in the Glory of the Garden."

Continuum

*This associative filament of letters, from Caroline Gordon to
Flannery O'Connor to John Hawkes to Joanna Scott to Scott's
student, Meg, suggests the legacy of generous analytic intelligence
that rescues writers from the solitude in which we must work; we
are, at our best—as the late, sorely missed Angus Wilson called
us—brothers and sisters in writing.*

Caroline Gordon

An accomplished novelist and short-story writer, the author of fifteen books, Gordon (1895–1981) was also a masterful investigator of other writers' fiction—see her work on Ford Madox Ford, *A Good Soldier,* and her *How to Read a Novel.*

Her generosity to Flannery O'Connor as she comments, with wonderful particularity, on the manuscript of what would become O'Connor's first novel, Wise Blood, *is stirring.*

Letter to Flannery O'Connor

St. Didacus' Day
[13 November] 1951

Your manuscript has come. I spent yesterday reading it. I think it is terrific! I know a good many young writers who think they are like Kafka. You are the only one I know who succeeds in doing a certain thing that he does. When I say that I am merely reaching out for some phrase that will partly convey my notion of your work. I do not mean that it is in any way derivative of Kafka. In fact, this book seems to me the most original book I have read in a long time. But you are like Kafka in providing a firm Naturalistic ground-work for your symbolism. In consequence, symbolic passages—and one of the things I admire about the book is the fact that all the passages are symbolic, like life itself—passages echo in the memory long after one has put the book down, go on exploding, as it were, depth on depth. As that old fool, E. M. Forster, would say: "You have more than one plane of action." (And what a contrast they are to the maunderings which he presents as *his* planes of action!)

Robert Fitzgerald reported to me something that you said that interested me very much, that your first novel was about freaks, but that your next book would be about folks. It is fashionable to write about freaks—Truman Capote and his followers write about little else. It astonishes—and amuses me—to find a writer like you using what is roughly the same kind of subject matter. But what a different use you put it to! Whenever I read any of the homosexual novels that are so popular nowadays I am reminded of something Chekhov said, that "he and she are the engine that makes fiction move." That strikes me as profoundly true. One can write

265

about homosexuals if one shows them as differing from normal people, as Proust does, but when a writer gives us a world in which everybody is a freak it seems to me that he is doing little more than recording the progress of his disease.

But homosexuality, childishness, freakishness—in the end, I think it comes to *fatherlessness*—is rampant in the world today. And you are giving us a terrifying picture of the modern world, so your book is full of freaks. They seem to me, however, normal people who have been maimed or crippled and your main characters, Sabbath, Enoch and Haze, are all going about their Father's business, as best they can. It *is* a terrifying picture. I don't know any other contemporary who gets just such effects. Genet achieves remarkable effects but for me they are all marred, finally, [by] his sentimentality. You are never sentimental.

I think that you have done a good job on the revision. I don't really see how you managed it. The Fitzgeralds told us that you have had a severe illness and are only recently out of the hospital. There comes a time for any manuscript when one must let it go with no more revisions. I think that having done the job you've done you could let this manuscript go with a good conscience. But I am going to make a few suggestions and comments. They are really suggestions for your future work, but I have to have something to pin them to, so I am going to take passages from "Wise Blood" as illustrations of the points I am trying to make. If I seem overly pedantic it is doubtless the result of teaching. When you are reading a manuscript for a fellow writer you can say "I like this" or "I don't like that" and he figures it out for himself, but if you are dealing with students you have to try to relate your reactions to some fundamental principle of the craft.

I admire tremendously the hard core of dramatic action in this book. I certainly wouldn't want it softened up in any way. I am convinced that one reason the book is so powerful is that it is so unflaggingly dramatic. But I think that there are two principles involved which you might consider.

It is the fact that in this world nothing exists except in relation to something else. (I take it that being a Catholic you are not a Cartesian!) In geometry a straight line is the shortest distance between two points. Theology takes cognizance of a soul only in its relation to God; its relation to its fellow-men, in the end, helps to constitute its relations with God. It seems that it is the same way in fiction. You can't create in a vacuum. You have to imitate the Almighty and create a whole world—or an illusion of a whole world—if the simplest tale is to have any verisimilitude.

As I say, I admire the core of dramatic action in this book very much, but I think that the whole book would gain by not being so stripped, so bare, by surrounding the core of action with some contrasting material. Suppose we think of a scene in your novel as a scene in a play. Any scene in any play takes place on some sort of set. I feel that the sets in your play are quite wonderful but you never let us see them. A spotlight follows every move the characters make and throws an almost blinding radiance on them, but it is a little like the spotlight a burglar uses when he is cracking a safe; it illuminates a small circle and the rest of the stage is in darkness most of the time. Focussing the reader's attention completely on the action is one way to make things seem very dramatic, but I do not think that you can keep that up all of the time. It demands too much of the reader. He is just not capable of such rigorous attention. It would be better, I think, if you occasionally used a spotlight large enough to illuminate the corners of the room, for those corners have gone on existing all through the most dramatic moments.

What I am trying to say is that there are one or two devices used by many novelists which I think you would find helpful.

Often one can make an immediate scene more vivid by deliberately going outside it. A classical example is the scene in Madame Bovary in which Charles and Emma are alone together for the first time. Charles' senses are stirred by Emma, he is looking at her very intently. At the same time he hears a hen that has just laid an egg cackling in a hay mow in the court-yard. Going outside that scene somehow makes it leap to life. The very fact that the sound is distant makes the people in the room seem more real. Hart Crane uses the same device in a poem called "Paraphrase." A man is standing beside a bed looking down at the body of a dead woman and grieving for her death. His grief is made more real by "the crow's cavil" that he hears outside the window.

I think that this very device could be used very effectively in "Wise Blood." Occasionally you get a powerful effect by having the landscape reflect the mood of the character, as in the scene where the sky is like a thin piece of polished silver and the sun is sour-looking. But it seems to me monotonous to have the landscape continually reflecting their moods. In one place I think you could get a much more dramatic effect by having it contrast with them. For instance, in the scene where Haze, Sabbath and Enoch meet, I think that the landscape ought to actually play a part in the action, as it does sometimes in Chekhov's stories. If the night sky were beautiful, if the night were lyrical the sordid roles the characters have to play would seem even more sordid. After all, here are three young people trying to do as best they can what they feel that they ought to do. Sabbath wants to get married.

Enoch wants to live a normal human life. Haze, who is a poet and a prophet, wants to live his life out on a higher level. You convey that admirably, I think, by emphasizing his fierce dedication to his ideals. But the scene itself is too meagre for my taste. Your spotlight is focussed too relentlessly on the three characters.

There is another thing involved: the danger of making excessive demands on the reader. He is not very bright, you know, and the most intelligent person, when he is reading fiction, switches his intellect off and—if the author does what he is trying to do—listens like a three or thirteen year old child. The old Negro preacher's formula for a perfect sermon applies here: "First I tells 'em I'm going to tell 'em, then I tells 'em, then I tell 'em I done told them." It takes much longer to take things in than we realize. In our effort to keep the action from lagging we hurry the reader over crucial moments. But anything that is very exciting can't be taken in hurriedly. If somebody is killed in an automobile accident, people who were involved in the accident or who merely witnessed it will be busy for days afterwards piecing together a picture of what happened. They simply couldn't take it all in at that time. When we are writing fiction we have to give the reader ample time to take in what is happening, particularly if it is very important. The best practise, I gather, is to do the thing twice. That is, the effect is repeated, but is so varied that the reader thinks he is seeing something else. Actually the second passage, while it interests the reader, exists chiefly to keep him there in that spot until he has taken in what the author wants him to take in. Stephen Crane uses this device often and to perfection in "The Red Badge of Courage."

Yeats puts it another way. He says that in poetry every tense line ought to be set off, that is, ought to be preceded and followed by what he calls "a numb line." He is constantly doing this in Major Robert Gregory. His numb lines do not slow up the action. They make it more powerful.

I am going to take an example from "Wise Blood," page 140. The place where the patrolman has just pushed the car—the pulpit!—over the embankment.

The paragraph: "Them that don't need a car, don't need a license" etc. is admirably concise. But I think you need another stroke or two in the next paragraph. I don't see Haze plainly enough. The chief thing I have learned from Flaubert is that it takes at least three strokes, three activated sensuous details to convince us of the existence of any object. I want to know how Haze's face looked then. His knees bending and his sitting down on the edge of the embankment is fine, but it is not enough for me.

Also I want to know how the patrolman looked when he said "Could I give you a lift to where you was going?" If we are to believe that anything happened we must be able to visualize the action. The minute we are unable to visualize it we quit believing in it. Very often a scene in which two people figure will be unconvincing because it is lopsided. The writer furnishes us the data which will enable us to visualize the main character but he doesn't give us the data that we must have in order to visualize the subordinate character. But he is there, taking up just as much space as the main character, and I think that he must be presented with just as much care. If, for instance, the main character is doing all the talking the reader's attention must be directed to the subordinate character at regular intervals. The fact that he isn't talking must be dramatized almost as much as the fact that the other man is talking—or you will get a one-sided affair. This whole passage is too hurried for me. It needs more sensuous detail and more numb lines. I want again to see how Haze's face looked when he said he wasn't going anywhere and again I want to know how the patrolman looked or at least what position his body assumed when he said "You hadn't planned to go anywheres?" A few, a very few more strokes would do wonders for that passage.

There is another thing that I think the book needs: a preparation for the title. Henry James says that at the beginning of every book "a stout stake" must be driven in for the current of the action to swirl against. This stout stake is a preparation for what is to come. Sometimes the writer prepares the reader by giving him a part of what is to happen. Sometimes he conveys the knowledge symbolically, sometimes he does it by certain cadences, as in "A Farewell to Arms," when at the beginning the narrator says "The leaves fell early that year"—another way of saying "My love died young." At any rate, however it is done, the reader must be given enough to go on, so that, in the end, he will have that comfortable feeling that accompanies "I told you so!"

I don't think that your title is prepared for enough. And this brings me to a consideration of Chapter V. I think that there is too much statement in this chapter. This is the only part of the book where you rely on statement rather than rendition. I *think* it is because you are uncomfortably aware of the difficulty of putting over Enoch's conviction that he has "wise blood." (It's a hellishly difficult problem!) I don't think you handle it quite right. You rather give your show away beforehand. That is, you tell us what Enoch did every day before you show him in the act of doing it. If you sum up what is going to happen before it happens the reader is not interested in it when it does happen. You tell us about his spying on the woman in the bathing suit beforehand. When he does spy on

271

her it's not very dramatic. But suppose you had prepared a little for your wise blood in previous chapters, say when Enoch and Haze first meet. Enoch is impressed by Haze. It is Haze's idealism, his fierceness, his latent power that impresses Enoch. But suppose Enoch let drop a few words to the effect that he, too, has a secret power? Maybe several times. This would be a dramatic rendition of the effect Haze has on him, which, I think, would be all to the good. It would also be a preparation for what is to come. He would not reveal what his secret power was at the time, beyond using the phrase "Wise Blood," but the reader would be on the lookout to find out what it was. Then, you could start Chapter V with action. That is, you could show Enoch to us in action, and refer to his "wise blood," and could inform the reader that he did certain things every day after showing him in the act of doing them instead of killing our interest by telling us about them beforehand.

To sum up, there are three places in the book where I think a few strokes might make a lot of difference, this scene and the scene where the patrolman pushes the car over and the scene where Haze and Sabbath and Enoch first meet.

And one more thing: I think you are just a little too grim with Sabbath when she is nursing the mummy. I don't like the use of the word "smirk" there. It is almost as if the author were taking sides against her. I think it would be more dramatic if you were a little more compassionate towards her. After all, she is a young girl trying to lead a normal life and this is the nearest she'll ever come to having a baby—since she'll probably end in the Detention Home. At any rate, the situation is grim enough without the author's taking sides.

I will now—God help us both!—make a few, more detailed comments.

I think that you overdo the summing-up of Mrs. Hitchcock's remarks. You sum them up half a dozen times. This would be more effective if you alternated direct quotation occasionally. I think that perhaps her first remark ought to be direct quotation. Reporting what she says there takes away from the immediacy of the scene and you are out to establish that.

You attempt to create Haze's eyes by two strokes. I don't think that it can be done. I have thought about this business of three strokes being necessary to create the illusion of life and I've come to the conclusion that it's related to our having five senses. A person can get along without one or more of his senses but once he's deprived of all of them he's dead. Two strokes is like a person who is deaf and dumb and blind and has, perhaps, lost his sense of touch to boot. He's hardly there.

Another thing. You begin and end the book with his eyes. This is one of those places that mustn't be hurried over. In fact, it might be well to do it twice, that is, in two ways. Mrs. Hitchcock ought to spend more time over his eyes so that the reader, looking over her shoulder, will also tarry there long enough to realize that they are, indeed, very peculiar.

Page 2 "yellow rock head." You or I might say that a man had "a yellow rock head," but the omniscient narrator, who is speaking now, can't say that. He speaks and writes Johnsonian English.

Page 2 "moved on him" isn't very good. Not exact.

3 Flaubert made it a practise never to repeat the same word on one page unless it was a word like said or did, a colourless word. Those two "flats" bother me.

5 When Haze says "I reckon you think you been redeemed" I think you ought to tell us what Mrs. H. said and how she looked. "Seemed confused" is too far away from the action, too much like reporting rather than rendering. We want direct action here.

6 I think you slip up a little on your viewpoint here. You haven't established the fact that we are seeing things through Haze's eyes and yet you use words he would have used: "the headman," for instance. I think it would be better to stick to the viewpoint of the omniscient narrator here.

6 Similarly, I think it would be better to say "the woman" Mrs. H. was talking to, rather than "the lady." The Om. Nar. would not call her lady. In his sight all women are equal.

7 "Squinched" is not good usage. The omniscient narrator doesn't ever use words like that.

7 "The knobs framing her face were like dark toadstools." In fiction "did" is always better than "was"—unless you are handling some state or condition so that mere being becomes a form of action. It seems to me that the toadstools ought to *frame* her face instead of just being.

9 Same thing goes for the sentence: "In his half-sleep he thought where he was lying was like a coffin." "Was" makes it less dramatic there. If I were doing it I'd say, "he thought that he was lying in a coffin." I'm not sure, though, that I'm right here. Maybe not.

13 "He had all the time he could want to be converted to nothing in" is another place where I think you hurry the reader too much. After all, his conversion to *nothing* is the crux of the book. You must give us time to take that in.

14 I don't like "The army had released him etc." You set the scene in one time then shift to another. Confusing. Why not "When the army released him a hundred miles north of where he wanted to be, he went immediately etc."

14 I'd say "glare-blue" instead of "the glare-blue."

14 I wish we could see the house from the outside, the figure it cut on the landscape, before he goes inside. Again, you go too fast.

17 I need to see the inside of that toilet. The scene would be much more real if we could see what it was like before you begin telling us of his situation: "He had no place to go," for instance. The fact that you haven't set your stage properly, haven't showed us what the little room looked like, takes away from the drama of this scene, which otherwise would be one of your best.

18 You have not taken the trouble to create the driver of the cab. I think that if a man sells somebody a newspaper in a story that man must be rendered. That is, the reader must be given just enough details to enable him to visualize the man. Otherwise you will have what Ford Madox Ford used to maintain was the most dreadful ghost story he knew: the guest in the country house who decides he will smoke in the night and is pretty upset when an unseen hand hands him a match. Anybody would be and anybody is when this happens. One gives a character like this a different kind of attention from the kind one gives important characters. Nevertheless, one must give him his due or he will take his revenge.

18 Here a device is needed that I think you had better get

on to. It is dangerous, I think, to have a character emit more than three sentences in one speech. If he does you get an unlifelike effect. If he has to say more than that you ought to dramatize the fact that he is making quite a long speech. Ordinarily, one can improve dialogue tremendously by making three speeches out of every speech. Thus:

Haze: "Listen, I'm not a preacher."

Then the driver either says something or doesn't say anything. In either case, the reader must learn how he received what Haze said.

Then we ought to know how Haze looked when he makes his next speech: "I don't believe in anything."

Again, we ought to know how the driver received that or what he said.

Then Haze says "I don't have to say it but once to nobody."

When speeches are run together in one paragraph the way you have Haze's remarks here they muffle each other. Speeches need air around them—a liberal use of white space improves almost any dialogue. White space at the end of a paragraph gives a speech room to reverberate in and if you will clear the space for it [it] will reverberate every time.

I think you have improved the scene where Haze meets Mrs. Watts but I think it still goes too fast.

The first paragraph on that page surely should end with Haze's picking her foot up and moving it to one side. But you have tried to handle Mrs. Watts in the same paragraph. You can handle only one idea in any one paragraph, just as you can handle only one main idea in any one sentence. A paragraph, like a sentence, is a miniature story and like a story, must always have a climax, must stop on the important note.

I want to know how Mrs. Watts looked when she drawled "You hunting something?" The fact that I can't see her makes it hard for me to believe that she said that. Also, I think that this is a place where you need white space. I'd break this up, like this:

Show how Mrs. W. looked, then have her say "You hunting something?"

Show how Haze receives this, then have him say "I'm no goddamn preacher."

Then show Mrs. Watts again and have her say something.

Then show him again and have him say "I've come for the usual business." I think then that your ending would work, all right. But as it stands, this passage goes so fast and is, besides, so meagre, that it isn't as convincing as it might be.

24 The omniscient narrator doesn't use expressions like "green-peaish colour."

50 I believe that the name of the shrub is lobelia. At any rate, I don't think "obelia" is right.

59 "There were two black bears in the first one." Why "were"? Why not make it did instead? "In the first cage two black bears sat etc."

62 Your use of a colloquialism like "squinched" in the crucial scene when they see the mummy lowers the tone of the whole scene.

62 I think that you should let the woman come in the door instead of telling us that Haze saw her. It would be more dramatic.

64 I think that your statement that he began preaching that night is giving the show away. Show him in the *act* of beginning his preaching and let the reader be the one to say "Oh, he began preaching that night." If you sum up what he does before he does it nobody wants to see him do it.

Also, if he is going to preach he's got to have somebody to preach to. "People" won't do it. You can't see, touch, taste, smell or hear "people" in general. You ought to create one, two or even three people who will stand for the rest of the crowd. But if he talks he's got to talk to somebody.

Also at the beginning of this chapter is a time when I'd like to know what kind of night it was. You go into your action too fast.

On page 67 you handle three or four ideas in one paragraph: Haze and the girl. Her father. His starting of his church. Won't work. That ought to be broken into several paragraphs, with, perhaps, a little more material worked in, a little amplification.

74 I think this scene ought to be broken up, too. For my students, I have fallen into the habit of making this sign [four underlinings] for such a breaking up and all through this letter I've found myself wanting to make that sign.

Each remark he makes in this passage ought to be in a paragraph by itself, accompanied by a rendering of how he looked when he said it. Also you ought to interpolate paragraphs showing how she received his remarks. If you did that you'd get the feeling of tension between two people. As it is, it goes too fast to be very lifelike.

Well, that's enough of that! I *would* like to see you make some preparation for the title, "Wise Blood," and I'd like to see a little landscape, a little enlarging of the scene that night they all meet, and I'd also like to see a little slowing up at certain crucial places I've indicated, but aside from those few changes I don't think that it matters much whether you make any of the revisions I've suggested. I am really thinking more of the work you'll do in the future than of this present novel which seems to me a lot better than any of the novels we've been getting. But of course in writing fiction one can never stand still. Once you learn how to do one thing you have to start learning how to do something else and the devil of it is that you always have to be doing three or four things at a time.

I have taken illustrations for the points I want to take out of your book. I might almost as easily have taken them from my own most recent novel, "The Strange Children." I am far enough away from it now to see some of the most glaring faults. One of them is the very thing I have been harping on all through this letter: hurrying over crucial moments too fast. My story purports to be the story of something that happened to a child and it is that story on one level of action, but it is also and chiefly, I think, a story of what happened to her father. In the first part of the story the child seems nearer to her mother. She goes to look at the waterfall with her mother but she looks at the stars with her father. Halfway through the book there is a shift of the emphasis from mother to father. When she falls off her pony it is her father who picks her up and at the last she is standing beside her father, with his arm around her. I told them, but I didn't tell them that I was going to tell them or that I had done told them. I should have forced the reader to linger long enough to realize that the emphasis was shifting from the mother to the father. As a result, few readers get it. But a few more strokes, a sort of holding up of the action long enough for the reader to be *made* to realize that something important was going on would have done the trick. Well, hindsight is always better than foresight.

You won't, of course, pay too much attention to anything I've said in this long letter. After all, it's just one novelist talking about the way she thinks things ought to be done. I may be quite wrong.

But my heartiest congratulations to you, at any rate. It's a wonderful book. I've written to Robert Giroux, expressing my admiration. My best wishes to you. I do hope that you continue to feel better.

Yours,
Caroline

Next morning:

I realize that in all this long letter I've said little about what I admire in the book. It is, first of all, I think, your ability to present action continually on more than one plane. Only writers of the first order can do that. Everything in your book exists as we all exist in life, mysteriously, in more than one dimension. When Haze runs the car over Solace Layfield he is murdering his own alter ego as well as Layfield. His Essex is not only a means of locomotion. It is a pulpit. When he finds out that Sabbath's father is blind he finds out much more than that. This goes on all through the book and yet you never succumb to the temptation to allegorize. I admire, too, very much, the selection of detail. You unerringly pick the one that will do the trick. And the dialogue is superb. But you will have gathered, by this time, that I am tremendously enthusiastic about the book. My heartiest congratulations on the achievement. It is considerable.

Yours,
Caroline

Flannery O'Connor

As celebrated for the slightly crazed light her clear prose offers upon her driven characters as she is for her uncompromising vision of humanity in the hands of a demanding, distant God, O'Connor (1925–1964) made dark, post-Faulknerian comedy from the life of the modern South. Her books are *Wise Blood, The Violent Bear It Away, A Good Man Is Hard to Find, Everything That Rises Must Converge,* and *The Collected Stories* of 1971. Her *Mystery and Manners,* edited by Sally and Robert Fitzgerald, as well as *The Habit of Being,* her letters, edited by Sally Fitzgerald, are valued for their commentary on writing.

Here, O'Connor responds with cordiality to John Hawkes, who once told this editor that "I wasn't aware that I had any influences," but who, if he was not influenced by O'Connor, was surely in tune with her affection for gothic imagery and the tracking of dark, psychosexual forces. The mutual respect between these fine writers is exemplary.

To John Hawkes

9 October 60

This is about how much I like *The Lime Twig*. It came last Sunday and I read it that afternoon and evening in a sitting that was unwillingly interrupted once or twice. The action seems to take place at that point where dreams are lightest (and fastest?), just before you wake up. It seems to me that you have retained all the virtues of the other books in this one, but added something that will hold the reader to the reading. I can't make any intelligent comments about this book any more than I could about the others; but I can register my sensations.

You suffer this like a dream. It seems to be something that is happening to you, that you want to escape from but can't. It's quite remarkable. Your other books I could leave when I wanted to, but this one I might have been dreaming myself. The reader even has that slight feeling of suffocation that you have when you can't wake up and some evil is being worked on you. I don't know if you intended any of this, but it's the feeling I had when the book was happening to me.

I want to read it again in a month or so and see if the second time I can take it as observer and not victim. Meanwhile my admiration is 90% awe and wonder. . . .

Again my admiration. Nobody else writes like you do.

John Hawkes

A master of lyrical prose threaded through with menace and hallucination, Hawkes (1925–1998) was a great challenger of the conven-
tions of the novel. He created beauty while generating fear and nervous laughter, in a career that lasted from 1949 to 1998. His novels
include *The Cannibal, The Lime Twig, Second Skin, The Blood Oranges,
Travesty, Adventures in the Alaskan Skin Trade,* and *Whistlejacket.*

*As his comment to his Brown University M.F.A.
student Joanna Scott suggests, Hawkes had a great
feel for the roll and twist of American English.*

Letter to Joanna Scott

October 25, 1984

Well, Joanna, I can't tell you how remarkable I find this story and how baffling! I don't actually know where it's set (some rural part of America where "English" or Scottish dialects are still prevelant? a sort of West Virginia?), and the story is so submerged that finally I'm not sure of the simplest narrative basis for this quite wonderful monologue-story: I don't know whether Gibble operates a bar or luncheon, don't know whether Gibble and the narrator actually had some sort of experience together on a raft built by Gibble, or whether the narrator's wife was on the raft (the entire raft sequence was one of the most puzzling of all). More important, I don't know if the wife is going off on the day of the monologue to have another operation or whether she is leaving the narrator husband—or he her—or whether at the end the wife is dying. Perhaps I'm again pressing unreasonably for literalness, clarity, but perhaps—and perhaps is the word—the reader deserves a clearer understanding of the situation. Toward the end the narrator begins to shift from "you" referring to wife to himself, or so it seems to me, or to the reader, and then suddenly begins to refer to her as "she": perhaps I've missed something, perhaps these changes in address and "distance" are functional, meaningful, but I thought them again puzzling and jarring. But the story, as I see it, is an amazing view of a marriage of 53 years between a man who loves and knows nature (the details are incredibly accurate) and a mailorder wife procured for him by Gibble—the separation between husband and wife, the power of the narrator's tenderness, the remarkable episode of the squirrel (dramatizing the narrator's childhood fears—of sex?—and need for love?) are all resonant with a kind of poetic wisdom. I confess that I don't understand the basic situation/idea of the story: that the wife, at least to the narrator, came to him as a kind of fallen woman/sexual allure, something to entrap the victim-fish. Is his view of her "correct"? Do we need a little more on her sex-manipulation, the sex fears she inspires (is all this my projection??), or is the "sex-lure" idea mainly the narrator's view and not necessarily perceptive? The nagging, the misunderstanding, the silence the narrator faces, his quandary of marriage, wife, husband is superbly dramatic. I still think that the wife is dying at the end, though I don't know where the operation comes in. Of course the main thing here is the remarkable language (that sent me scurrying to the dictionary more than once!) which seems to be a mixture of formal archaic diction, and some sort of syntactically disrupted regional or local dialect: it's superbly sustained, and even though I can't place it or entirely understand it at times, still it creates its own drive, reality, and becomes the voice of an isolated man in a way I've not quite come upon before. (Is this voice/language in fact invented? perhaps the question is irrelevant). At any rate I think this story could stand as it is, or deserves minor clarifications, or might really need a little more narrative situating. The pleasure of it is considerable. . . .

Jack

Joanna Scott

Scott is the author of four novels (*Fading, My Parmacheene Belle; The Closest Possible Union; Arrogance; The Manikin*) and of a collection of stories (*Various Antidotes*). She teaches at the University of Rochester.

Watch a word from her teacher, John Hawkes, surface after thirteen years as Scott, teaching, passes along a crucial concern.

Dear Meg

Dear Meg,

The density and stretch of your prose is exciting. You want to make the language intelligent, provocative, challenging. But you need to keep it *intelligible*. The metaphor of the womb is used and reused in this fiction, but I don't understand the multiple meanings. What do you mean by "She can hear the movement of their throats, feel the vibrations of crimson colored uvula, the left over sentiment of New York." What do you mean by "Scratching at the wall of merciless sound to make a place"? Actually, more often than not it's a redundancy in the meaning, not an elusiveness, that troubles me in this piece. You give us a sense of despair early on; New York is dreary, dirty, stale. Rain does not purify. So why repeat this effect? And why do you need to keep reusing the metaphor of the womb? If you're suggesting that her return to her lover's apartment is some kind of birth, this could be explored more directly, with more self-consciousness. And do you really want the political implications of "The screams of abortion clinics, pathetic weeping that hope goodbye can be heard by the ears of bloody tissue fragments." For some readers (for me, I should say) this overshadows the metaphorical insinuations, and the fiction starts to seem a vague attack on abortion. Is this what you're intending? If so, make the politics clear. If not, change the line.

I've tried to mark the lines that are weakened by repetition or drift off into description that strains for effect. There are stunning, provocative passages here (the expression of love, for instance). Why not make the whole piece stunning and provocative? Push for clarity, Meg—then your ideas will have an irresistible force.

Permissions